ALSO BY JASON NEAL

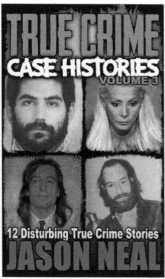

Please also check out the other volumes of this series

http://truecrimecasehistories.com/series/

THANKS!

Thanks for purchasing True Crime Case Histories Volume One. I'm currently working on future volumes with more disturbing true crime stories.

I encourage you to sign-up for my free email list for updates, discounts and freebies on all of my future books.

http://truecrimecasehistories.com

Thanks,

Jason Neal

CONTENTS

CHAPTER INDEX

James Patterson Smith - A young girl in England tries to hide her relationship with a much older man from her parents, but ends up being tortured and mutilated for three weeks before she is killed.

Fred Grabbe - A Midwest farmer decides it's better to kill his wife and burn her body than get caught in an affair and give up ownership of the farm.

Murder of Elaine O'Hara - A truly unbelievable story of a suicidal woman and the dark secret of her master/slave relationship gone horribly wrong.

The Toolbox Killers - Two psychopaths who never should have been let out of prison terrorize the Los Angeles beach towns in the 70s with their torture and murder of young girls.

Chris Coleman - The story of a bible-thumping idiot that kills his wife and two young boys to avoid losing his job over his affair.

INTRODUCTION

A quick word of warning: the short stories within this book are unimaginably gruesome. Most news stories and television crime shows tend to leave out the most horrible details about murder, simply because they are too extreme for the general public.

I have done my best to include full details of these stories, no matter how sickening they may be. In these true crime stories, you'll find that truth really is stranger - and vastly more disturbing - than fiction.

In my first book, I've started with a few of the stories that have haunted me for some time. Some of these stories are unbelievable in their brutality, while others are astounding in the stupidity of the perpetrator.

You'll find a story of a religious evangelical who would rather strangle his wife and two young boys than lose his prominent job with the church.

Then, there's the story of a man that fills his wife's orifices with grease so she'll burn from the inside.

There's the story of the small-town doctor that goes to unbelievable lengths of performing surgery on himself to avoid going to jail for raping his patients.

Plus, there're more stories of serial killers terrorizing cities and investigations that bring seasoned crime scene officers to tears.

These stories are from all around the globe and have no common thread between them, other than that they are both thought provoking and disturbing.

The stories included in this book are dark and creepy, and will leave you with a new understanding of just how fragile the human mind can be.

-Jason

JAMES PATTERSON

On an April afternoon in 1996, a man calmly walked into a Manchester police station in England to report that his girlfriend had accidentally drowned in his bathtub. The man was forty-eight-year-old James Patterson Smith and his girlfriend was just a seventeen-year-old child. The truth was that Smith was a sadistic, controlling psychopath and not only had the girl drowned, but she had been subjected to three weeks of some of the most brutal torture England had ever seen. The horrific crime scene brought seasoned police officers to tears.

Kelly Anne Bates was mature for her age. At age fourteen when Kelly told her parents, Margaret and Tommy Bates, that she had a boyfriend, they thought nothing of it. As any parent would, they assumed it was a teenage crush with a young boy from school.

Wanting to raise their children with a sense of independence, they gave Kelly a long leash and let her see her boyfriend as she pleased. It wasn't long before Kelly started staying out overnight and her worried parents called police. When Kelly finally came home, she told them she was staying at her friend Rachel's house, but her parents had a sinking feeling that her story wasn't true.

They weren't the only one concerned about Kelly's where-abouts. Even though they had never met him, Kelly's boyfriend "Dave" would occasionally call to ask where she was. What her parents didn't realize at the time was that Dave was already tightening his control around Kelly.

Kelly managed to keep her parents from meeting Dave for a full two years, until she was sixteen years old. That's when she informed them she was dropping out of school and moving in with him. Her parents were livid and called social services and the police for help. Because Kelly was now sixteen, according to UK laws the authorities couldn't do anything. Kelly's parents demanded to meet her boyfriend, Dave.

When Margaret and Tommy finally met him, they were shocked to find that Dave was not a boy but a full-grown man. Kelly and Dave told her parents that he was thirty-two years old, but even that wasn't true. They later found out he was actually forty-eight - older than Kelly's father at the time.

Dave's age wasn't the only thing they were hiding from her parents. Dave was not "Dave" at all. His name was actually James Patterson Smith.

Though mature for her age, Kelly was still young and naïve. She was flattered to have an older man so interested in her, but what she didn't realize was that their relationship was more about power and control than love. Smith controlled everything the young girl did from this point on.

Kelly's demeanor slowly changed. She was no longer the

bright, bubbly girl that her mother knew, and they gradually saw less and less of her. When she did show up at her parents' home, she seemed to be troubled and depressed, but refused to admit anything was wrong.

Kelly would show up with bruises on her arms and face. When she showed up with the whole side of her face black from bruising, her parents' concerns reached a new level.

Kelly lied to her mother and told her that she was jumped by a group of girls that beat her up. Each time she showed up with new injuries, her story would change. Her parents had no idea that Smith had a long history of violence towards young women.

Margaret could clearly see this was abuse and went to the police, who told her to make an appointment with a doctor and get Kelly to go in for an exam, so they could document the abuse. But again, Kelly was sixteen and considered an adult. Her mother was helpless. Unless Kelly went in of her own accord, there was nothing that could be done.

Kelly's mother could see that the violence was escalating when Kelly showed up with a horrible bite mark on her arm. Again, Kelly shrugged it off and said that she fell and caught her arm on a chain-link fence.

In November 1995, Margaret pleaded with her to leave Smith, but this seemed to anger Kelly. She then told her mother she would be seeing much less of her. That was actually the last time Margaret saw Kelly alive.

Over the following months, Kelly phoned her mother and told her that she had gotten a job at a factory and was working long hours and weekends; that was why she hadn't come around. Eventually, the phone calls stopped.

In March 1996, Margaret got a Mother's Day card and a birthday card for her father, Tommy. Both were clearly not written in Kelly's handwriting. Smith was now in complete control and toying with them.

On April 17, 1996, James Patterson Smith walked into the Gorton Police Department and reported that his girlfriend had drowned in his bathtub. Police arrived to a horrific bloodbath that was obviously much more than a drowning.

Seventeen-year-old Kelly Anne Bates had indeed drowned in the bathtub, but she had also been held prisoner for at least three weeks and suffered torture beyond imagination.

The pathologist's report revealed 150 separate injuries, including having her eyes gouged out, stab wounds inside her eye sockets, and the mutilation of her mouth, ears, nose, and genitalia. Her head was partially scalped, she was scalded with boiling water, burned with a hot iron, stabbed and cut with knives, forks, pruning shears, and scissors, and her knees had been kicked in.

Literally every room in the house had traces of Kelly's blood. Evidence revealed that she had been tied to a radiator by her hair and her eyes were gouged out at least a week before her death. She had not received water for several days and had been starved, having lost about forty-five pounds.

Investigations revealed that there was a progressive pattern with Smith. They found that he had been married years before and divorced due to his violence against his wife. After the divorce, he dated a twenty-year-old who testified that he used her as a "punching bag" even while she was pregnant. Their relationship ended when he tried to drown her. After that, he had a relationship with a fifteen-year-old girl who testified that he held her head underwater.

At the trial, Smith denied the murder charges and believed he was justified in his torture. Smith claimed that Kelly taunted him about the death of his mother and that she only had herself to blame. He also claimed she had, "a habit of hurting herself to make it look worse on me." When asked why he gouged her eyes out, he said, "She dared me to do it."

The jury didn't even need a full hour to come back with a guilty verdict. The evidence and photos seen at the trial were so horrific that, after the trial, the jury was offered psychological counseling. Every jury member accepted.

James Patterson Smith was sentenced to life imprisonment with a minimum term of twenty years. Kelly was buried the day before her eighteenth birthday.

2

FRED GRABBE

The Grabbe family was wealthy, by small town standards. They were easily one of the wealthiest families in Marshall, Illinois, a tiny farming town just ten miles from the Indiana border. Most of their wealth came from the inheritance that Charlotte Grabbe had acquired from her parents.

Both Charlotte and her husband Fred were extremely hard workers. They worked long hours farming their soybean and corn fields, but their life was far from perfect.

The couple had two children, Jeff and Jennie, and when there were problems between their parents, the kids usually took Charlotte's side. Fred and Charlotte had been married for twenty-three years filled with violence- so much so that they had divorced once and remarried, but the second marriage looked to be headed toward divorce as well.

Fred was an extremely large man standing at six foot four, while Charlotte was petite. During their heated arguments, Fred had no problem using his fists on his tiny wife or his son, Jeff. Things had gotten so bad that Charlotte had instructed Jeff and Jennie to come looking for her if she wasn't back to the house by the end of the work day.

Fred was also a serial philanderer and, at forty-two years old, had a fascination with younger women. Usually having a few girlfriends on the side at any given time, Fred was currently dating a twenty-four-year-old, curly-haired, blonde bartender named Vickie McAllister.

After learning of Fred's latest affair, Charlotte filed for divorce and Fred moved out of the family home into a cabin on the family farm. Jeff and his wife moved into the main family house with Charlotte.

Shortly after Fred moved into the cabin, Charlotte filed battery charges against him after he assaulted her when she went to the cabin to take some furniture back to the main house.

A little after sundown on July 24, 1981, Charlotte hadn't returned to the house. Jeff and Jennie knew something was wrong. She had gone out to the soybean field on her tractor but hadn't returned by sundown, so they went looking for her. Later that evening, they found the tractor she had been driving parked inside a machine shed with her lunch box still resting on the front tire. Jennie immediately went home and reported her mother missing to the Clark County Sheriff.

When questioned by the Sheriff, Fred admitted they had a quarrel, but said the last time he saw her she was driving her car toward the interstate highway.

A few days later, Charlotte's car was found in Terre Haute, Indiana, just 16 miles away, across the state border. Police searched her vehicle and found no blood or signs of foul play, but they did find a loaded handgun beneath the seat.

Contrary to Fred's story, a friend of Charlotte's came forward and told the Sheriff she saw Fred driving his truck towards Terre Haute with someone following in Charlotte's car. Someone other than Charlotte. They claimed the person driving Charlotte's car was a young, blonde woman with curly hair.

Investigators found that Charlotte had placed notes in a safe deposit box at the local bank just ten days before she went missing. In those notes, she wrote that she thought Fred was stealing farm equipment, and that she didn't think she would live through a divorce. She said she was afraid of Fred and his business partner, Dale Kessler. The Sheriff questioned Dale Kessler who claimed Fred was with him on the evening Charlotte went missing.

At Jeff and Jennie's request, the Sheriff brought Fred and Vickie McAllister before a grand jury, but both of them refused to talk, invoking their Fifth-Amendment rights. Jennie even asked her father to take a lie detector test to prove he didn't kill her mother. He refused.

Charlotte's case went cold for three years. Jennie and her husband offered a $1,000 reward for information. They later raised it to $10,000. Then again to $25,000, but nobody came forward.

Eventually Jennie hired a private investigator, Charles Pierson.

Pierson decided to follow the clue of the curly-haired blonde driving Charlotte's car. Clearly, Pierson believed the woman driving the car was Vickie McAllister and he wanted to talk to her.

Pierson heard that Fred and Vickie had broken up and she was now living in West Terre Haute, Indiana. Pierson said,

"There seemed to be two things she liked to do. Drink beer and play pool. So, I started going to bars in the area and doing both. I met her, and we became friendly."

When Pierson finally admitted to her who he really was and why he befriended her, she couldn't help herself but to spill the beans. He said the information just poured out of her, like she really needed to get it off her chest. The secret she had been holding inside was eating her alive, and she was more than willing to come clean.

McAllister admitted that she was the one driving Charlotte's car that day. That was just the beginning. She went on to describe the gruesome details of what happened that night and the following day.

Vickie McAlister's story made her physically ill each time she told it. The story would eventually be told to authorities and, later, to two juries.

McAllister recalled that she was with Fred Grabbe in the machine shed that day to get some fifty-five-gallon metal barrels to use for farm work. As they were getting the barrels, they heard Charlotte's tractor and Fred told Vickie to hide behind another tractor inside the shed.

Fred went outside of the shed to meet Charlotte when they got into a heated argument. The argument escalated as they came back inside the shed. Eventually, Fred couldn't control his rage and began strangling her. Using his bare hands, he choked her neck until the point she was almost unconscious. He then released and let her regain consciousness. Then choked again. He would repeat this over and over again until eventually he choked his wife to death.

Once Charlotte was dead, he then sodomized her lifeless body while Vickie watched. Fred then grabbed a grease gun from the shed and filled all of Charlotte's orifices with grease. He crumpled her body into one of the 55-gallon barrels and loaded the barrel into the back of his pickup truck.

Grabbe instructed Vickie to drive Charlotte's green Ford LTD that was parked outside and follow him as he drove his truck across the state line into Indiana.

That night, they dumped Charlotte's car outside of a bar in Terre Haute and then drove back to Grabbe's farm and parked near the Wabash River. Grabbe took the barrel out of his truck and placed it near a maple tree, where he poured diesel fuel in the barrel covering Charlotte's body. He then lit it on fire. Fred and Vickie sat on the riverbank while the barrel burned. The diesel fuel and the grease inside her body burned slowly all night long.

The next morning, they heard the search party approaching so they put out the fire, loaded the drum back into Fred's truck with Charlotte's charred body inside, and headed back to Vickie's home.

At sunset that night they went back to the river, put the barrel in the same spot, and set it ablaze again. Again, it burned all night. In the morning, Fred rolled the barrel into the river. The only body part remaining was Charlotte's skull, to which he said, "This will make good fish bait" as he threw it into the river.

Vickie's confession helped, but it simply wasn't enough. Prosecutors needed some sort of physical evidence to charge Grabbe. With no body, no barrel, and no murder weapon, investigators need something besides Vickie McAllister's word against Fred's. Officially, Charlotte was still just a missing person.

The new Sheriff in Clark County was Dan Crumrin, and he was curious if the maple tree that still stood above the burn site could somehow be used. Crumrin asked the University of Illinois for help and they sent a plant biologist, Eugene Himelick, and an organic chemist, Donald Dickerson.

During the natural cycle of a tree's life, the seasons will cause a tree to grow in the spring and summer, then go dormant in the winter. This process each year creates the familiar ring in the trunk and branches of every tree. A ring in the tree's branch will show the growth of that year.

Diesel fuel is highly toxic to a tree and, if it doesn't kill the tree, it will at the very least hamper the growth.

Himelick and Dickerson took samples from the branches of the maple tree. Their findings concluded that three rings deep (meaning three years ago) the growth of the tree was much thinner. The tree had gone through some sort of stress the summer that Charlotte went missing.

They then took the samples and shredded them into sawdust, which Dickerson analyzed using a Gas Chromatograph Mass-Spectrometer. A Mass-Spectrometer is a device that identifies the components of a sample, even in very tiny amounts.

In their analysis they found the presence of hydrocarbons found in diesel products. There were a total of five branches tested. The two branches located on the side of the tree that the barrel was on showed the hydrocarbons. The other three on the opposite side did not.

This forensic evidence was enough to convict Fred Grabbe. One of the prosecutors used in the trial was Robert Egan of Chicago. Egan had been the prosecutor on the trial of John

Wayne Gacy, a serial killer convicted for the murders of thirty-three young men in 1980.

Fred Grabbe was found guilty of first-degree murder and sentenced to life in prison without the possibility of parole. However, this story is far from over.

During the trial, Fred had the support of his latest girlfriend, Barbara Graham, a twice-divorced mother of three from a nearby town. Fred had purchased her a mink coat that she wore in the courthouse during the trial to torment the family.

A few weeks after Grabbe's conviction, he was being held in the Clark County jail when Barbara Graham attempted to break him out. Barbara showed up at the jail and told Deputy Sheriff Mike Paulson that she wanted to give Fred a love note. When Paulson opened the door she fired five shots, one hitting the Deputy in the leg. She then hovered over him and said, "Don't make me kill you." Graham's attempt, however, was unsuccessful. She was sentenced to 16 years in prison for that crime. The judge that sentenced Grabbe to prison was convinced that Fred had somehow planned the breakout attempt from behind bars.

Just two months later with Fred still in prison, the Grabbe home and the home that Fred's son, Jeff, had built nearby both burned to the ground. Fire Marshalls determined that both fires were intentionally set. Police suspected that Fred had something to do with it from prison, but since he was already serving a life sentence, they didn't pursue it.

During Fred's imprisonment, his lawyers filed an appeal of his verdict and got his first conviction overturned on a technicality. By this time, Vickie McAllister was living another life under another name, but she came back to Clark County to testify against Fred once again.

Just a month before the second trial, Fred's son Jeff, who had testified at the first trial, had vanished. He was on a business trip in California when all family members lost contact with him. By the time of the trial date, Jeff was nowhere to be found. The judge allowed his wife Cindy to testify in his absence. Despite Jeff's absence, Fred was again convicted a second time and sentenced to seventy-five years in prison.

One month after the trial, Jeff's body was found floating in the water at Seal Beach in California. Three bullet holes riddled his body, and an anchor was tied around him to keep the body down. To this day, Fred denies having anything to do with his son's murder.

Vickie McAllister received the $25,000 reward that Jennie and her husband had offered and was relocated under yet another assumed name. She still lives in fear that Fred will somehow find her from behind bars.

As of 2018, Fred Grabbe is inmate number N57941 at Menard Correctional Center in Centralia, Illinois. He is eligible for parole in 2022.

In yet another strange twist to this family story, years later in 2014, Fred's grandson, Adam Everett Livvix was indicted on weapons and immigration charges in Netanya, Israel. He was suspected of impersonating a Navy SEAL and plotting bombing attacks on Dome of the Rock, an iconic mosque in Israel. Livvix was diagnosed as being psychotic and unfit to stand trial. He was held in a mental institution in Israel for a year before he was released back to the US where he faced charges of stealing farm equipment.

3

THE MURDER OF ELAINE O'HARA

On the evening of August 22, 2012, Elaine O'Hara went missing near Dublin, Ireland. What happened that day, and the investigation over the next three years, proved to be one of the most shocking crimes in Irish history.

On the morning of August 23, Sheila Hawkins planned on taking her partner's daughter, Elaine O'Hara, to the Tall Ships Festival in Dublin before she went to work for the day. Elaine had volunteered to work at the festival weeks before and was quite excited to attend.

When Elaine didn't show at their meeting point that morning, Sheila contacted Elaine's father, Frank. Frank assured her that Elaine had probably driven herself to the festival and forgot to let her know. He assured her everything was ok and not to worry about it. Regardless, Sheila went to Elaine's house and rang the doorbell. When there was no answer, she left for work.

Frank had spent the prior day with Elaine after she was released from St. Edmonsbury Hospital. Elaine had spent three weeks there for her problems with depression. After leaving the hospital, Elaine and her father had lunch where she talked about the Tall Ships Festival. Frank recalled that she was clearly excited to be a volunteer. Later, they drove to visit her mother's grave. During the drive Frank noticed Elaine texting someone, but he had no idea who. After an emotional visit to her mother's grave, Elaine went home around 4 p.m. to prepare for the festival the next day.

Later that day, there was still no word from Elaine. Knowing Elaine's history with depression and self-harm, Frank decided to use his key to check on her apartment. Nothing in the apartment seemed out of place, but Frank became worried when he noticed that Elaine's iPhone was there. Still, thinking it might be an accident, he left her apartment and waited.

Elaine had a history of psychological problems dating back to her early teens. During school she was a victim of bullying and, when one of her closest friends died in a car crash, Elaine attempted to take her own life by slashing her wrists.

Despite her fulfilling work with children, throughout the years she struggled with her depression. It reached a pinnacle when her mother died in March 2002 and Elaine was hospitalized again. By 2003 she seemed back on track, but it was short-lived. Dr. Anthony Clare, her psychiatrist whom she had grown close to, died in 2007 and this was another huge setback for Elaine.

Dr. Clare had diagnosed Elaine with depression and border-line personality disorder. She additionally suffered from asthma, diabetes, and dyslexia. Dr. Clare said Elaine possessed a childlike innocence and was emotionally submissive, with the emotional maturity of a 15-year-old. He also noted that Elaine had developed an obsession with being restrained, imprisoned, and punished, so much so that it had become a sexual fantasy.

Dr. Clare initially diagnosed her with gradually emerging psychosis. He later changed the diagnosis to borderline personality disorder and depression. Elaine was prescribed heavy depression medications and tranquilizers, to the point where her father would notice her falling asleep while eating dinner. Frank later recalled that Elaine had lost much of her late teen and adult life to medication and hospitals.

Throughout the years following her mother's death, Elaine was hospitalized a total of 14 times for depression and suicidal tendencies.

In July 2012, just six weeks before her disappearance, Elaine was once again contemplating suicide and checked herself into St. Edmonsbury Hospital. During her stay, the hospital staff recalled Elaine talking constantly about the Tall Ships Festival. She was planning to volunteer her time for a full week and was clearly excited to attend.

By the end of her stay at St. Edmonsbury, Elaine's new psychiatrist, Dr. Murphy, had reduced her medications significantly. He said that, despite her struggles, 2012 was a good year for Elaine. She was discharged with no indication of suicidal tendencies.

Frank had agreed with the doctor. Elaine had seemed to be doing better, but with her sudden disappearance, he just couldn't get the idea out of his head that she may have done something horrible to herself.

Later that evening, there was still no word from Elaine. Frank sent her a text, "Are you still alive?" There was no response to his text message. Elaine's sister called her phone. Again, no answer.

The following morning, Frank and Sheila still hadn't heard from Elaine and decided to go check her apartment once again. When they arrived nothing had changed from before, but now they also noticed that Elaine's handbag was still there. This was something he had missed when he was there before. This was deeply troubling; Elaine would never leave her phone and her handbag. Sheila then reached into Elaine's laundry basket and found a latex bondage suit and mask. Out of privacy for Elaine, she initially hid her finding from Frank. He was already upset, and this would have just troubled him more, so she decided not to mention it yet.

Frank and Sheila had known of Elaine's obsession with restraint and bondage since her teenage years, but they had no idea how far her fantasy and gone.

Frank checked the hospital to see if Elaine had possibly checked herself back in again, but she hadn't. The next logical spot to check was to go back to the Shanganagh Cemetery. Elaine's brother-in-law, Mark Charles, drove to the cemetery where Elaine often went to visit her mother's grave. That's when he spotted her little turquoise Fiat. They contacted roadside assistance to get into her car where they found two packs of cigarettes, a lighter, her driver's license, a portable satellite navigation system, and a mobile phone charger that wasn't for an iPhone. To the best of their knowledge, the family only knew Elaine to have one phone - an iPhone.

Knowing that Elaine had a history of suicide attempts, and Shanganagh Cemetery was just a short walk to the sea, Frank was extremely worried that Elaine had taken her own life.

Now panic stricken, the family conducted a more extensive search of her apartment. There, in addition to her iPhone, handbag, and latex suit, they found all of her medication for

anxiety, depression, diabetes, asthma, vertigo, and choles-
terol. There were also pages she had printed from a hunting
website detailing two types of hunting knives. She had also
printed maps of the Killakee Forest and the Vartry Reservoir.
The Killakee Forest was a large wooded area located adjacent
to the Shanganagh Cemetery where her car was found. The
Vartry Reservoir was about twenty miles away. In Elaine's
desk, they found a notebook with website addresses for
alt.com and |CollarMe.com. Both were sexual fetish
websites.

The next morning on August 24, with still no word from
Elaine, Frank O'Hara went to Garda, the National Police
Force in Ireland. Police headed to the cemetery to investigate
the car, the cemetery, the nearby fields and forests, and the
shoreline but found no clues. They attempted a search by
helicopter, but bad weather wasn't cooperative.

Police then focused their attention on Elaine's apartment.
Her apartment complex had 10 security cameras in various
spots throughout the property. Elaine was seen leaving her
apartment at 5:05 p.m. on the 22nd, just thirty-six minutes
after she arrived home after visiting with her father. She was
wearing what looked to be navy colored track suit bottoms,
white running shoes, and a blue hoodie. She was also
carrying a telephone which clearly was not her normal
iPhone. Her friends and family only knew her to have the
one phone and this was particularly puzzling.

Police again went back to the cemetery and the adjacent park
to do further searches. While in the park they came across a
jogger, Connor Gilfoyle, and showed him a photo of Elaine.
When asked if he recognized Elaine, he said he had encountered her just a few days ago. Gilfoyle had been trying out an
app on his phone called MapMyRun that day, so he was able

to use it to give police the exact location and time that he encountered her in the park. He saw her at 5:45 p.m.

Gilfoyle mentioned that Elaine seemed a bit tense and preoccupied. She had asked him if he knew the directions to a footbridge that crossed the railroad tracks and led toward the beach. When he told her he didn't know, she didn't say thank you. She just walked away. 30 minutes later, he saw her again on the other side of the footbridge, so he knew she made it to the bridge.

Police and family members walked the beach for hours but found nothing. Both the police and family assumed the worst; that Elaine had taken her own life. Her case was officially listed as a missing person. One year later, the family laid flowers in her honor at Shanganagh Cemetery next to her mother.

The summer of 2013 was very hot. A heatwave that swept Ireland that year had dropped the water levels in the Vartry Reservoir from twenty feet down to almost one foot. On September 10, 2013, William Fegan, his brother, and a friend were fishing from Sally's Bridge when they noticed something shiny beneath the surface of the water. When they fished it out of the water, they found handcuffs, clothing, a ball gag, restraints, and leg restraints. At the time, they thought it was a bit amusing and they left the items on the bridge. The next day, Fegan was a bit troubled by the items and decided to bring them to the Roundwood Garda station.

Garda officer James O'Donahue treated the BDSM (bondage, domination, sadism, and masochism) items as if they were evidence, but at the time he had no idea if a crime was even committed. He let the items dry out, bagged them, and tagged them. O'Donahue thought "Why would someone dispose of these in a reservoir? If it's just a couple disposing of their adult toys, why not just throw them in the rubbish? Someone was trying to hide something."

The following day, O'Donahue went to the spot where Fegan found the items to search the area more thoroughly. Unfortunately, the water was murky that day due to high winds, so he decided to try another day. On the third trip to the area, Officer O'Donahue searched through the silt and found more handcuffs, an asthma inhaler, and a set of keys. On the keyring were two supermarket loyalty cards, one of which was for a local store called Dunne Stores.

On September 16, 2013 O'Donahue contacted Dunne Stores to find out the identity of the owner of the loyalty card. They reported that it belonged to Elaine O'Hara. O'Donahue wasn't familiar with her missing persons case until he ran her name through the police computer. What was happening at the same time just twenty miles away was an unbelievable coincidence.

Magali Vergnet was a professional dog trainer and regularly walked her dogs through the Killakee Forest. On August 21, 2013, her personal dog, Millie, a King Charles Cavalier Spaniel, emerged through some dense brush with a bone in her mouth. Magali thought nothing of it, assuming it was an animal bone and set the bone on a stack of bricks nearby and continued on her way. Over the next several weeks Millie continued to go into this same dense brush and emerge with a bone in her mouth. Finally, on September 13, 2013, Millie didn't return from the bushes and Magali went in to find her. When she found Millie, she also found a ribcage of bones. Magali still assumed they were animal bones until she came across the leg of a tracksuit pant. She touched the pant leg with her foot and realized there was also a running shoe. She immediately left and called the property owner who then contacted the police.

The police searched the area further and found 65 percent of a human skeleton, including a jawbone and a shovel. When DNA and dental records were searched it was confirmed that they were the remains of Elaine O'Hara.

It was September 17, 2013, one day after Officer O'Donahue had positively identified the BDSM items and supermarket loyalty cards as belonging to Elaine O'Hara.

Police then conducted a much more comprehensive search of the reservoir. They recovered a red and black backpack, leather mask, multiple knives, various BDSM items, eyeglasses, and two Nokia phones. The phones looked similar to what Elaine O'Hara was seen holding on the security camera from her apartment. The eyeglasses had a serial number on them which identified them as purchased from a store called Specsavers. Further investigation revealed the prescription was that of Elaine O'Hara.

Police had a forensic computer team search Elaine's computer and found that she frequented dating sites that catered to the BDSM world: Alt.com and CollarMe.com. Computer forensic specialists found that she had talked to several users on these sites, but one username in particular stood out - Architect72. The messages between them referenced "cutting myself" and "punishment involving a master's scalpel." Architect72 was also linked to a gmail account with the username "fetishboy."

Elaine had confided in friends and family members that she had been having a BDSM relationship with an architect, but her friends knew nothing about him other than that he was married.

Unbelievably, the two Nokia phones both powered on after more than a year submerged in the reservoir. Each phone only had one contact; one with MSTR and the other with SLV, clearly "Master" and "Slave" with the vowels removed. What they found on the phones was quite disturbing. Thousands of text messages spanning several years between the two that revealed a very dark relationship.

MSTR: "I'm a sadist. I enjoy others' pain. You should help me inflict pain on you and help me with my fantasies,"

MSTR: "I want to stick my knife in flesh while sexually aroused... blood turns me on and I'd like to stab a girl to death."

MSTR: "If you ever want to die, promise me I can do it"

MSTR: "My urge to rape, stab and kill is huge. You have to help me control or satisfy it"

MSTR: "Every time I stab or strangle you, I want you to think this is it and every time I let you live, you owe me your life and are grateful and worship me,"

MSTR: "Either you let me stab you or you help me do it to someone else.

MSTR: "Lots of people have stabbed and got away with it, why not me?"

SLV replied several times that she was frightened and didn't want to talk of killing or blood anymore.

SLV: "I'm too young to die"

SLV: "you have this hold over me that terrifies me."

SLV: "I'm just so scared. Do you know, sir, that I'm scared of you? You have this hold over me"

SLV: "I know my life is in your hands... every time we meet,"

SLV: "Please don't mention killing for a while, just until I settle back into life"

The phone number for MSTR was cross-referenced with the contacts on Elaine's iPhone and it matched a contact named David. Investigators called the number but there was no answer.

Investigators found that the cell phones were "burner phones," disposable phones purchased at a store in Dublin under the fake name Goroon Caisholn. They did, however, find someone with a very similar name, Gordon Chisholm, and brought him in for questioning. After questioning, police realized this was not their man.

While poring over the text messages, police finally got a potential break.

SLV: Went well today sir, I take it you are now a daddy again thanks for last night sir, really needed it.

MSTR: Yes, beautiful baby girl (child's name excluded). glad you enjoyed the other night, many more sessions to come, see you sometime over the weekend.

Those texts were from March 31, 2011. Police now knew that MSTR had a newborn baby girl born on that day. And they knew her name.

Another clue they got from the texts was:

MSTR: "...came fifth in flying"

This one was dated June 11, 2011. Police initially thought he was possibly a pilot or maybe it was a reference to fly-fishing, but after searching competitions around that time they soon realized he was referring to model airplanes. He had apparently come in fifth in a model airplane flying competition.

Roundwood Model Aeronautical Club had a competition during that time and the person that came in fifth was named Graham Dwyer. Coincidentally, when looking further into Dwyer's background, they found that he had just had a baby born earlier that year.

During this same time, Detective Chief Superintendent Diarmuid O'Sullivan received a tip from a confidential informant who claimed that they knew who killed Elaine O'Hara. The tipster pointed to an architect named Dwyer. Graham Dwyer.

Police now knew they had their man.

Superintendent O'Sullivan found Dwyer's house and, during the night, took his garbage from the curb. Police went through the trash and from the contents were able to put together a DNA profile of Graham Dwyer.

In Elaine's apartment her mattress had puncture marks, possibly from a knife, plus blood and semen stains. Forensic technicians were able to get DNA from the semen stains which didn't match anything in the police database, but did match the DNA acquired from Graham Dwyer's trash.

On October 17, 2013, police knocked on Graham Dwyer's

door. There was no answer, so they went to the side door and Dwyer answered in his pajama bottoms and no shirt.

Graham Dwyer was a family man: a seemingly respected architect working in Dublin whose hobbies were fast cars and model airplanes. None of his friends, family, or co-workers knew of his double-life. Dwyer lived with his wife and two young children in Foxrock, a quiet suburb of Dublin. To the majority of the world, he was just an average guy, but it's now obvious that the life he displayed was a charade. To look at him, you would never imagine such a monster could lurk behind his eyes.

Dwyer wrote to his wife from his jail cell and insisted to her that he did not murder, "that awful woman." His wife subsequently left him.

The trial was one of the biggest in Ireland's history. The story dominated headlines because of Dwyer's seemingly normal life.

The amount of evidence that piled up after the extensive investigation was overwhelming.

The security cameras from Elaine's apartment showed Dwyer visited the complex nine times between January and August 2012. On July 9, it showed Elaine with him entering the elevator shortly after 5 p.m. and Dwyer leaving forty minutes later. Footage on August 13 and 15 showed Dwyer carrying a bag similar to the bag found in the reservoir.

Elaine's internet search history revealed searches for, "Graham Dwyer Architect."

Gordon Chisholm, the man who was originally suspected because his name resembled the name the phones were purchased under, Goroon Caisholn, ended up being an old acquaintance of Dwyer.

Even Dwyer's own son pointed him out in the security footage from Elaine's apartment complex.

Dwyer's personal phone was turned off between 5 p.m. and 9 p.m. the night Elaine went missing. On Dwyer's computer there was an online order on August 17, 2012, for a hunting knife that was delivered to his work address on August 21, the day before Elaine went missing.

Additionally, there was erotic horror found on his computer and he had shared files with her about stabbing and killing. His computer also had videos that he had filmed of himself and four women, where he is seen stabbing the women during sex acts. Many of the videos featured Elaine O'Hara.

Several of the texts from Dwyer matched his personal life. He often mentioned his children by name, spoke of the birth of his daughter, and also referenced the Polish embassy that he visited for his architectural firm. There were further references to tattoos, car repair bills, purchasing a bicycle ("to get fit for murder"), and the 15 percent pay cut that he received at work. Everything from the texts synched perfectly from Dwyer's real life.

Despite the ridiculous amount of evidence against him, Dwyer still insisted he was innocent.

The courtroom was filled on January 22, 2015, when the trial began. The defense tried to argue that all of the evidence was circumstantial and called only three witnesses. The prosecution called 194 witnesses, including Dwyer's wife who testified that the shovel found with Elaine's remains was from their garden. Gemma Dwyer recognized the shovel because it had orange paint splatters on it from when they painted their garden fence at their home in Foxrock.

Additional witnesses included Dwyer's former partner and mother of his adult son, Eimear McShea. She described him as controlling and abusive and had the desire to stab her during sex. She testified that he asked to bring a knife into the bedroom. She eventually agreed to his request, as long as he kept it on the side table. but Dwyer just couldn't control himself and had to hold it while they had sex.

Darci Day, a young American woman that Dwyer had chatted with online, testified by video link. Darci testified how he confided his fantasies of killing Elaine O'Hara. "He said he used to cut her… in the stomach area and stuff. That it was mutual and sexual… He basically wanted to go after her and, if she wanted to, he wanted to kill her and come after me."

Photoshopped images on Dwyer's computer showed Darci laying topless with her throat slit and her intestines coming out of her stomach. Police also found a document of fiction titled "Killing Darci" in which he fantasized about stabbing the American woman to death while they had sex.

Still, Dwyer's defense team claimed that, because pathologists did not determine a cause of death, that there is no evidence that implies that Dwyer was responsible for Elaine's death. They argued that she had been released that morning from a psychiatric hospital for having suicidal thoughts and even her own family believed she had taken her own life. They presented the case that the text messages the prosecution were using as evidence, were nothing more than sexual fantasies.

The prosecution, however, argued that the text messages

detailed a very specific plan for Elaine's death, and she had repeatedly asked "not to be stabbed" and "not to be beaten" by Dwyer. They argued that Dwyer knew she was being released from a psychiatric hospital, lured her to her mother's gravesite and the remote mountain area, knowing that the police and family would believe Elaine took her own life.

The trial lasted forty-five days and, on March 27, 2015, the jury of seven men and five women came back with a verdict. Guilty. Graham Dwyer was sentenced to life in prison. The judge said that he "agreed 110 percent" with the jury's decision. The trial was emotionally hard on the jury members and, because of this, the judge exempted them from further jury duty for the next thirty years.

If it weren't for the strange series of coincidences; the disobedient dog, the summer drought, etc. Graham Dwyer may not have been caught. It's still unknown who Chief Superintendent O'Sullivan's "confidential informant" was, as that evidence was not used in the trial.

The following is the final chain of text messages between SLV and MSTR sent between August 14 and 22, leading up to the death of Elaine O'Hara.

August 14

MSTR: "Am I right in thinking you don't want to die anymore?"

SLV: "I'm sorry I made you so mad."

MSTR: "You'll have to take a punishment. If anything happened to you, who knows about me?"

SLV: "No one knows your name, and no one knows about you really. They know I'm into BSM and that I meet people."

MSTR: "OK, let's keep it that way. If I ever meet your neighbour, I'm your brother, David, ok?"

SLV: "I already told the girl next door that you are a friend."

MSTR: "Would she make a good victim for me?"

SLV: "Too close to home,"

MSTR: "Ok. We will start going on outdoor walks for play and hunting."

SLV: "Sir, do I have to come?"

MSTR: "Yes, help me plan it. You won't be there… but I want to do it this year."

SLV: "Every time I think about it, sir, I want to heave,"

MSTR: "Just think about me being happy doing it. It's what I like. If you were any good, you would help me find her, hold her down while I kill her."

SLV: "Sir, are you going to stab me?"

MSTR: "Yes, I'm going to make you bleed. Nice and deep in your guts," August 16

SLV: "I am scared that the punishment will go on for a long time."

MSTR: "No. Swift and brutal. Might even kill you."

August 17

MSTR: "Did a huge walk up the Dublin Mountains yesterday. Plenty of lonely hill walkers up there."

August 20

MSTR: "Morning slave, looking forward to seeing you Wednesday."

SLV: "I'm not being stabbed,"

MSTR: "Ok, but you must take some sort of punishment."

SLV: "I know."

MSTR: "What kind of punishment would you like? Choices are hard anal with stabbing and choking. Whipping till bleeding. Chained overnight in a forest. Choked unconscious. If you don't pick one then it's all four."

SLV: "I don't know sir. Sorry doc came in. Sir u know I can't make choices."

MSTR: "Ok overnight in woods."

SLV: "Sir, I'll take stabbing."

MSTR: "Ok, but I must see blood… And I want to do it outdoors."

SLV: "Please sir, indoors."

MSTR: "Why?"

SLV: "I'm afraid if outdoors, you might kill me."

MSTR: "I won't kill you. If I was, it would be indoors hanging once you are chained up."

SLV: "I know, I mean that's it, nothing else?"

Elaine's next texts explain that she's planning on attending the Tall Ships Festival, so she asks:

SLV: "I was wondering if you could keep the visual marks to a min sir, please?"

MSTR: "That's a big request. But Ok."

SLV: "Thank you sir, I appreciate it. I can cover wrists and arms, it's the neck sir."

MSTR: "Don't worry. I won't stab you in the neck."

SLV: "Maybe not but you want to."

August 21

SLV: "R u mad at me sir?"

MSTR: "No but you must be punished for trying to kill yourself without me and for being unavailable for so long."

SLV: "Yes sir, I know. Master needs to punish slave."

MSTR: "I'm going to get blood on my knife for this a lot of blood then we can move on."

SLV: "Yes sir."

MSTR: "That's my good slave. Master is very horny and needs to put his cock in his slave."

SLV: "Master, may I ask you something?"

MSTR: "Yes, but don't upset me before I am about to cut you."

SLV: "Do you go by the Gorean way and is it just a fantasy? Gorean I mean?"

MSTR: "It's a real lifestyle that people really live by. Yes you are my slave but I need you to be serving me not stuck in a hospital. I wish I could fuck you on my lunch break."

SLV: "How do we do that master?"

MSTR: "You need to get out of hospital and serve me."

SLV: "Yes master im out tomorrow sir. It will be after lunch as the doc wants to see after lunch at 2.30 b4 I go."

Master then turns the conversation again to suicide.

MSTR: "Are u happy going on like this forever?"

SLV: "Sir, please stop. You want me to be in here forever! Can't we just have a normal master slave relationship without this please sir."

MSTR: "Ok but you must promise me next time you fall down that I end you. Hopefully you will be Ok though."

SLV: "Ok, I promise sir."

MSTR: "I mean it now. I will get into trouble if I don't do it at this stage."

SLV: "What do you mean? How could you get into trouble? It's suicide. It's fucking suicide. Don't be troubling yourself. It's suicide! No one will look into it."

MSTR: "I want to watch as well and be there for you so you won't be lonely."

SLV: "Shit. That's shit. I am lonely all the time and you're not there that's how I get like this. You just want a hard on. You're being fucking selfish!"

No reply from Master.

SLV: "Sir, sorry. Just get angry talking about it. I just want to try again. Be a good person/slave/friend and I want to try and have a normal life without talking and thinking about that. Please let me try."

MSTR: "Ok." Later that day…

MSTR: It's up to me and you have a big punishment coming up, getting knifed in the guts."

SLV: "I know sir. I better be tied up good sir. Please not outdoors, please."

MSTR: "I know. You will be well bound and gagged and tied to a tree deep in the forest. I have a spot picked out."

SLV: "What if we get caught?"

MSTR: "We won't get caught."

SLV: I'm not leaving my apartment. You will have to drag me out."

MSTR: "You will do what you are fucking told. I want outdoor play and you are going to follow instructions, or I will double punishment or hang you."

SLV: "How do you know we won't get caught."

MSTR: "I found a really, really remote place. No one will find us."

SLV: "Sir, do I have to be naked!"

MSTR: "It's very deep in the forest and yes you do. I don't want blood over your clothes."

SLV: "Now I'm terrified!"

MSTR: "Trust me it will be exciting."

SLV: "Sure sir. So what time do you want me tomorrow sir? I was going to go see my niece before I went home and they are hols (sic) next two weeks!"

MSTR: "5:30"

SLV: "Do I have to drive, sir?"

MSTR: "A bit, yes."

SLV: "Now, I'm really scared."

MSTR: "Don't be scared." Elaine reassured Dwyer that she hadn't mentioned him during any of her counseling conversations.

MSTR: "That's good. No one should know about me. They would still find me in your emails and way back in your alt history. So relax."

MSTR: "I'm heading to the spot now to double check."

August 22. The day of the murder.

SLV: "This place, although a pain in the ass at times, is safe because I know what's coming and I don't want to leave. I'm just so scared. Do you know, sir, that I'm scared of you? You have this hold over me.

MSTR: "Do not fear death."

SLV: "Please don't mention killing for a while, just until I settle back into life."

MSTR: "But, tonight's punishment will be like me pretending to do someone for real. It's important to me that you feel it's my right to take my slave's life if I want to. Every time I stab or strangle you, I want you to think this is it and every time I let you live, you owe me your life and are grateful and worship me."

SLV: "I know my life is in your hands… every time we meet," she wrote.

She texted around midday to say she had got out earlier than expected, was on her way home and to ask if he had any instructions.

MSTR: "Have a bath, make sure your cunt shaved, no underwear not even a bra. Loose clothes, footwear for mud. Make sure you are fed. Take painkiller,"

SLV: "Can I do what I want until I am needed?"

MSTR: "Like what?"

SLV: "I don't know yet, just anything I want to do."

MSTR: "You will be in a lot of pain later and next few days."

SLV: "It's going to be that bad? I'm going to be busy next few days. Tall Ships please don't make it really sore Please."

MSTR: "You will have stab wounds. You know the drill. The last few didn't bleed. These will."

SLV: "Sir how many?"

MSTR: "As many as I like."

SLV: "Yes Sir.

MSTR: "I want you to park at Shanganagh Cemetery at 5.30. Leave your iPhone at home. Just bring Slave phone and keys. You will get further instructions there."

SLV: "Sir are we doing this if it's raining? Are you coming back to my place? I need to clean, it's dirty."

MSTR: "Yes, if it's raining. No, I won't be back at your place."

SLV: "No offence sir, but do we have to do it in the rain. It's cold."

MSTR: "Don't worry, it's never as bad as u think it's going to be."

SLV: "Yes Sir."

MSTR: "Don't be nervous and enjoy being told what to do."

SLV: "Easier said than done sir."

MSTR: "Empty yourself and become nothing. You are property and a piece of slave meat. Your only job is to serve."

SLV: "Can I wear socks with runners? Can I bring inhaler? Didn't have time to eat, will we be late back?"

MSTR: "Yes to socks. Leave inhaler in car. You should be back at car abt 8. More painful getting stabbed on empty stomach. Suit yourself. See you in a bit. x"

SLV: "Here Sir."

MSTR: "Ok, take only keys and Slave phone. Make your way on foot to park next door and text me in the middle."

SLV: "Please let me take inhaler sir."

MSTR: "Ok."

SLV: "Ok sir is the park with the playing fields in the top part or bottom."

MSTR: "Ok cross railway bridge in the next park near cliffs."
SLV: "I'm lost I'm in the football field now."

MSTR: "Look for railway footbridge near footpath."

SLV: "Here now, where's park?"

MSTR: "Cross bridge and head for opposite end of park near steps to sea."

SLV: "OK on the footpath yes no?"

MSTR: "Yes."

SLV: "Steps here."

She texted him to say she was at the steps. Elaine received the final text at precisely 6 p.m. on August 22, 2012.

MSTR: "Go down to the shore and wait."

A total of 2,612 texts were sent throughout the years between those two phones and with this final text, Graham Dwyer then achieved his ultimate sexual fantasy of stabbing a woman to death presumably during sex.

The following is the "Victim's Statement" that was read in the courtroom after the conviction:

"We know that we are not the only victims of this crime. We recognize that other families are suffering too, and we feel for every other person affected. Words cannot adequately describe how we are feeling, and we would never want any other family to go through what we have endured over the past two and a half years.

We have lost a daughter, a sister and a friend in the most brutal, traumatic and horrifying manner.We also have many unanswered questions which we will have to carry with us for the rest of our lives.

Elaine was a very intelligent girl, who never fully realized her potential due to her psychological difficulties. She was prescribed a lot of medication and this did have an impact on her ability to be a regular teenager, particularly socially.

She was emotionally immature and very trusting of anyone who showed her kindness. In later years her medication was reduced, hospital stays became less common and she functioned more effectively. However, she had missed out on those important, formative teenage years.

She had a strong work ethic and loved working with children, as she could relate to them better than to adults. She was always there to help and assist others, giving lifts, covering shifts at work or collecting many of the items for the Christmas Fair at school.

Elaine adored her niece who was also her goddaughter and loved reading, painting and playing with her. For months after she went missing, her goddaughter would point out cars that were like Elaine's saying, "There's Elaine's car".

We smiled and nodded – how can you explain something to a young child that we couldn't understand ourselves? Since she left us, Elaine has two more nieces, but they will never know their aunt.

Elaine's ambition was to be a teacher and she was studying Montessori. In 2014, we collected a BA in Montessori education which was awarded to her in St Nicholas Montessori school. She would have been so happy and proud to stand up in her gown and hat to accept that degree herself after overcoming many obstacles to finally get the qualification she longed for, but unfortunately this was not to be.

When Elaine went missing in August 2012 we were devastated. At that time, she appeared to us to be progressing well in life. She had a new apartment, was studying and working in two jobs.

She had a setback in July of 2012 and was voluntarily admitted to hospital. However, on weekend release, she was in very good form and was looking forward to the future.

The assumed suicide in August 2012 was a surprise to all the family but lack of evidence pointing to any other cause for her disappearance meant we reluctantly needed to accept that she had most likely taken her own life around Shanganagh.

We spent many hours walking the shore from Blackrock to Bray searching for any sign of her. A year after her disappearance we laid flowers in the sea at Shanganagh in her memory and in an effort to find some closure for us as a family.

Our attempt at closure was premature as when in September 2013 Elaine's remains were discovered, the Garda investigation changed from that of a missing person to murder. This led to further anguish for the family as we now faced the imaginable horror of Elaine having been murdered.

The trial has been an incredibly difficult experience. It was distressing to see Elaine's private life laid bare before the nation, despite the fact that she was the victim. Some of the reporting in the print media was insulting to Elaine and deeply upsetting for the family. At times, Elaine's life was relegated to a lurid headline in a newspaper.

It was heartbreaking for us to listen to the texts Elaine received from a depraved and diseased mind. The manipulation of her vulnerability was apparent and when she tried to resist, she was reined back in.

We can hear her voice in those texts, just wanting to be loved. Hearing the contents of the videos will haunt us forever. We were upset that the credibility of our evidence was questioned, as throughout the two and a half years all we wanted was the truth and justice for Elaine.

We will probably never know what happened in Killakee on Wednesday the 22nd of August 2012, but there are questions that trouble us:

When did Elaine realise it was not a game anymore?

When did she realise that the intention was to kill her for real?

Did she try to run?

Was she restrained?

Did she suffer much?

Could she and did she cry out?

Was she left on the mountain to die alone?

This is OUR life sentence. For us there is no parole."

4

THE TOOLBOX KILLERS

The 1970s were a notorious time for serial killers in the Los Angeles area. There was the Night Stalker, the Freeway Killer, the Hillside Strangler, and many others. However, one of the most vile and disgusting killings were perpetrated by the duo of Lawrence Bittaker and Roy Norris.

Lawrence Bittaker had experienced trouble with the law since he was twelve years old. By the age of eighteen, he had dropped out of school and spent time in the California Youth Authority for shoplifting, petty-theft, auto theft, hit and run, and evading arrest. When he was released, he found that his adoptive parents had disowned him and moved to another state.

Within days of being released, Bittaker was already in trouble with the law again. He was arrested for stealing a car and driving it across state lines. In August 1959, he was sentenced to prison for ten months in Oklahoma and then transferred to Springfield, Missouri, but released the following year.

Bittaker developed a pattern of getting arrested, getting released, and getting arrested again. Over the next fourteen years he was arrested at least six times for offenses ranging through parole violation, theft, leaving the scene of an accident, burglary, etc.

During his incarceration, he was put through several psychological tests in which he was diagnosed as being borderline psychotic, a highly manipulative character, and having considerable concealed hostility. He was also found to have quite a high IQ of 138. Further examinations showed he was resistant to acknowledging his responsibility; Bittaker confided in his psychiatrists that his criminal activities gave him a sense of self-importance. He was prescribed anti-psychotic medications.

Finally, in 1974, Bittaker was caught stealing a steak from a supermarket. When the store clerk followed him into the parking lot to confront him, Bittaker stabbed him in the chest just missing his heart. Bittaker ran but was subdued by two other supermarket employees. The clerk survived and Bittaker was convicted of assault with a deadly weapon and sent to the California Men's Colony in San Luis Obispo.

Roy Lewis Norris lived part of his childhood with his birth parents, but occasionally was passed around to various foster homes throughout Colorado where he was a victim of sexual abuse by a Hispanic family he was living with. When he was sixteen, he made sexual references to a female relative. When he was punished for this, he stole his father's car and drove into the Rocky Mountains and attempted suicide by injecting air into his artery. He was caught by police as a runaway and returned home to the news that his parents were divorcing. They told him they were only married because of him and his younger sister, and they didn't want their children anyway.

At seventeen, Norris dropped out of school and joined the US Navy. At twenty-one he was sent to Vietnam. While there, he learned to become an electrician and started using heroin and marijuana.

In November 1969, Roy Norris was arrested for rape and attempted rape when he forced his way into a woman's car. He didn't spend much time behind bars and, three months later, he tried to break into a woman's home.

U.S. Navy psychologists diagnosed Norris with a severe schizoid personality and he was given an administrative discharge from the navy: "Psychological problems."

In May 1970 on the San Diego State University campus, Norris stalked a female student, attacked her, and struck her in the head with a rock. He pounded her head into the sidewalk while he kneed her in the back. Charged with assault and sentenced to five years at Atascadero State Hospital, he was diagnosed as a mentally disordered sex offender.

After five years, authorities determined he was "no further danger to others" and released him into the public. It only took three months for him to revert back to his perverted ways when he raped a woman in Redondo Beach. Norris was sentenced to California Men's Colony in San Luis Obispo, where he met Lawrence Bittaker.

While in prison, Bittaker had saved Norris from attacks by other inmates a few times and they had become friends. As they grew to know one another, they realized they had many common interests, mostly involving sexual violence toward women. The two discussed how they loved the sight of frightened young women. Bittaker, until this point, had not committed any sexual offenses but expressed his interest to Norris and stated, if he ever did commit such a crime, he would kill her. He said he wouldn't leave a witness to the crime.

During their time behind bars their friendship evolved, as did their plots for perversion. They discussed at length how, upon their release, they would fulfill their fantasies and rape and murder young girls. One for each age between thirteen and nineteen years old.

Bittaker was released first in October 1978. He was a skilled machinist and was earning $4,000 a month, quite a sum for that time and especially so for a convicted felon only a few months out of prison.

He was living in a Burbank motel and was very popular with the local teenagers. It was well-known that he always had beer and pot available.

Norris was released three months later in January and moved in with his mother in Redondo Beach. He started working as an electrician in Compton and it wasn't long before he got a letter from Bittaker. They met in February and planned their mayhem.

The first order of business was to buy a van. If you've heard the term, "serial killer van" this is possibly where the term came from. The duo purchased a 1977 GMC cargo van in February 1979, with no side windows and a large sliding door. Just like the cliché. They would nickname their killing machine "Murder Mac."

For three months, the couple cruised up and down the Pacific Coast Highway from Redondo Beach up to Santa Monica. Perfect Southern California weather and beach communities meant lots of young girls on their way to the beaches and, during that time, they would stop and talk to girls, offer them pot, offer them a ride, party, have some beer, and take Polaroid photos. It was all just a practice run for their bedlam. They picked up twenty girls just for the sake of practicing their routine; to get the girls into their van voluntarily.

Once they were confident that they could do this, they built a bed in the back of the van. Beneath the bed they stored a cooler with beer and soda to lure the girls, a toolkit for torture items, and clothes to change into after theirs were soaked with the blood of their victims.

Next, they searched for a location. Somewhere secure. Somewhere private. Just beyond the San Gabriel Mountains they found an old fire road. They broke the lock on the gate and replaced it with their own.

It was go-time. They were on the hunt.

June 24, 1979. Cindy Schaffer was just sixteen years old when her grandmother dropped her off at St. Andrews Church in Redondo Beach for a fellowship meeting. Cindy only stayed for twenty minutes and then decided to walk home.

On her walk home Bittaker and Norris pulled up to her and asked if she needed a ride. "No, thanks." They tried again and offered her some marijuana. "No, thanks." She kept walking.

They pulled up ahead of her and parked. Norris opened the sliding door to the van and pretended to get something out of the back. While she walked by, Norris grabbed her and threw her into the van. Bittaker cranked the stereo to full volume to muffle the screams while Norris gagged her and bound her feet and legs. This became their modus operandi of acquiring victims.

Bittaker drove the van up to the San Gabriel Mountains to their secret hideout. Once there, Norris told Bittaker he wanted some time alone with Cindy. Bittaker agreed and wandered off into the mountains while Norris raped her. During the night, the two took turns raping and torturing her. Cindy asked if they were going to kill her and Norris replied, "No." She then begged, "if you're going to kill me, please just let me pray." They declined her request.

Bittaker later recalled that Cindy "displayed a magnificent state of self-control and composed acceptance of the conditions of which she had no control. She shed no tears, offered no resistance, and expressed no great concern for her safety… I guess she knew what was coming."

When it came time to kill her, the two apparently argued as to who was going to kill her, both wanting the other one to do it. Norris lost and was chosen to finish the task. Norris tried to strangle her with his bare hands but, after forty-five seconds, became physically disturbed by the look in her eyes and released his grip. He ran to the front of the van and threw up, false teeth and all.

Bittaker took over. He tried to strangle her as well, but apparently strangling the life out of a person was much harder than either of them imagined. Cindy slumped to the ground and began convulsing. He then grabbed a coat hanger from the van and put it around her neck. With a pair of pliers, he began twisting the ends. Twisting and twisting until she eventually died.

Bittaker found a steep cliff and the two of them wrapped her body in a plastic shower curtain and threw her off. Bittaker assured Norris that the animals would eat any evidence of a body.

Meanwhile, Cindy's grandmother calls police when she doesn't arrive home, but without a body and no evidence of foul play, the police are at a loss.

Just two weeks later, on July 8, 1979, Bittaker and Norris were cruising the Pacific Coast Highway looking for their next victim when they spotted eighteen-year-old Andrea Hall hitchhiking in Manhattan Beach. As they slowed to offer her a ride, another car slowed at the same time and she got into their car instead. The two followed the car and, once the first car had dropped her off at Redondo Beach, they then offered her a ride and she accepted.

This time Bittaker was driving but Norris was hiding in the back, ready to strike. Once Andrea got in the van, Bittaker offered her a drink. When she accepted, he told her to go get one out of the cooler in the back. Norris lay in wait. Norris grabbed her and again, Bittaker turned up the volume on the radio while Norris tried to subdue her.

Andrea was a strong girl and put up quite a fight, but eventually Norris overpowered her, gagged her, and bound her wrists and ankles. All the while, Bittaker drove to their secret location.

Once they arrived, Bittaker raped her twice and Norris once. Norris thought he saw the headlights of a car so they decided they would drive further into the mountains and continue.

Andrea screamed and pled for her life but her cries only empowered them.

Bittaker forced her to walk alongside the van, naked, uphill, then preform fellatio and pose for Polaroids. Norris drove back to town to get alcohol and when he returned Bittaker had already killed her. He told her to give him as many reasons as she could to live, then he shoved an ice pick in each of her ears. That wasn't enough to kill her, so he strangled her and threw her over a cliff.

Andrea's sister and brother-in-law report her missing, but again, police had nothing to go on.

The killers took a two-month break and, on September 3, spotted fifteen-year-old Jackie Gilliam and thirteen-year-old Leah Lamp sitting on a bus stop bench near Hermosa Beach. The girls had been hitchhiking and Bittaker and Norris stopped to offer them a ride to the beach. The young girls accepted.

It wasn't long before Leah realized Bittaker was driving away from the beach, not toward it. Bittaker gave the excuse that they were looking for a place where they could park and smoke some pot. Leah didn't buy their story and reached for the sliding door and tried to jump out. Norris had a bag full of BB's and quickly hit her over the head with it and threw her back into the van. When a bystander at the public tennis courts noticed the altercation, Bittaker told the man she was just having a bad LSD trip, and they drove off.

Bittaker drove back to their private location and the two started the chaos. Neither of them was interested in Leah because they thought she was overweight and instead they focused on Jackie. Bittaker took out his cassette recorder because he wanted to record his first rape of a virgin. He commanded Jackie to pretend like she was enjoying it. Norris went one step further when he raped her and told her to pretend like he was her cousin.

That night, Norris and Bittaker took turns standing watch while the other slept next to the girls. In the morning they took Leah up a hill and told her to strip naked. They then took photos of her in sexual positions, tied her up, and left her.

Bittaker again turned his focus back to Jackie and shoved an icepick into her head and strangled her, just like he did to Andrea.

Leah again tries to escape, but before she could, Bittaker struck her in the head with a short-handle sledgehammer, knocking her out. He then strangled her. To make sure she was dead, Norris beat her in the head.

Both girls were reported missing by their families, but like the girls before them, police had no bodies and nothing to go on.

Another two months passed, and the two men were out on Halloween when Bittaker saw a girl he knew. Sixteen-year-old Lynette Ledford was standing outside of a gas station. She had left a Halloween party in Sunland-Tujunga near Los Angeles. She had fought with some boys at the party and was now headed home; Bittaker offered her a ride. Bittaker was a regular at the McDonald's where she worked, so she accepted the ride.

Bittaker was impatient and, rather than drive to their fire road location, he decided to do this one on the move. He drove down a deserted suburban street where Norris drew a knife. He then bound and gagged her with duct tape.

The two men switched places and Norris drove aimlessly around the streets for over an hour. Bittaker, in the back with Lynette, carried out their most vicious rape yet. Bittaker turned on the tape recorder to record everything while he beat her, raped her, and forced her to fellate him. He forced her to say that she liked it through the cries and screams. He then ripped apart her clitoris, rectum, labia, and nipples with a pair of pliers from his toolbox.

By the time it was Norris' turn to rape her, there was nothing left but bleeding orifices. He forced her to fellate him while he beat her elbow over and over again with a sledgehammer. Norris encouraged her to scream louder and louder. He beat her twenty-five times on the elbow and each blow can be heard on the recording along with her blood-curdling screams.

The tape recorder is turned off and Norris strangles her to death with a coat hanger, twisting it until it was only slightly larger than a silver dollar.

> "We've all heard women scream in horror films ... still, we know that no-one is really screaming. Why? Simply because an actress can't produce some sounds that convince us that something vile and heinous is happening. If you ever heard that tape, there is just no possible way that you'd not begin crying and trembling. I doubt you could listen to more than a full sixty seconds of it." - Roy Norris describing the recording of that night.

Believing they were above the law and immune to prosecution, Bittaker decides to dump the body publicly. He chose a random residential front yard to dump the body. He wanted to see the reaction of the public and authorities when the body was found.

A jogger found the body early the next morning with the coat hanger still around her neck. The press, police, and Los Angeles residents were terrified. The murder hunt began, but it would be three weeks before they would get another clue.

The next month, Roy Norris visited an old friend from the California Men's Colony, Joe Jackson. Norris had spoken to Jackson in the past about his fantasy of raping young girls. Norris felt comfortable talking to him about his exploits with Bittaker since their release. He included all the graphic details of the most recent victim, Lynette Ledford. At this time, Lynette's was still the only body that had been found.

Jackson was an ex-convict, but he was also the father of two young girls. The gruesome details of Norris and Bittaker's killings did not sit well with him. Jackson contacted his attorney who, in turn, informed the police. The case was assigned to Detective Paul Bynum of the Hermosa Beach Police Department.

The police brought Jackson in for questioning and he told Bynum about the van. His description of the van matched a description given by a girl that had been raped two months prior. The victim of this rape, Robin Robeck, now lived in Oregon. Detective Bynum revisited Robin, and she immediately picked out Norris and Bittaker from a photo lineup.

Roy Norris was put under surveillance and was easily caught when officers could see him from the street weighing marijuana and putting it into baggies for sale. Police arrested Norris on parole violations of possessing drugs and dealing marijuana.

Police searched a car that Norris owned and found photos of young women, but Norris claimed none of those girls were harmed.

That same day, while the police were still at Norris' home, Bittaker called and an officer answered the phone. Pretending to be one of Norris' friends, the officer tried to lure him in, but Bittaker with his 138 IQ didn't fall for it. He immediately drove to a cemetery in the Hollywood Hills and buried the torture tapes. He then returned to the motel room in Burbank where he was living and was immediately arrested.

Bittaker was surprisingly cooperative when arrested and handed over several Polaroid photographs. Many of the photos were of Andrea Joy Hall and Jackie Gilliam.

Both men initially claimed to be innocent, but when police found the van, there was just too much evidence to deny. They found over 500 photos of young women, two necklaces from the victims, a book on how to find police broadcasting frequencies, a sledgehammer, a jar of Vaseline, a plastic bag full of lead weights, and, most damning of all, a tape from the final killing of Lynette Ledford. The tape was played for Lynette's mother Shirley and she confirmed it was her daughter's voice.

In Bittaker's motel room investigators also found seven bottles of acidic liquids. The killers apparently had plans to step-up their game with the next victims.

Detective Bynum and Deputy District Attorney Stephen Kay interrogated Roy Norris. When faced with the mounting evidence, Norris decided to take a plea deal. He pled guilty for his role in the killings and agreed to testify against Bittaker. In exchange, he was offered a reduced sentence, meaning no death penalty nor life without parole. Bittaker, however, admitted to almost nothing.

Bittaker was charged with five counts of first-degree murder, robbery, kidnapping, forcible rape, sexual perversion, and criminal conspiracy. Norris was charged with the same, except one of the first-degree murders was reduced to a second-degree murder charge.

Norris then led investigators to the fire road in the San Gabriel Mountains. He showed them exactly where each killing took place. During the interrogation, Norris spoke of the murders, "in a casual, uncoerced manner" like a mechanic would explain a problem with your car. No emotion at all.

Upon searching the San Gabriel Mountains, police were able to recover the bodies of Jackie and Leah, but the bodies of Cindy and Andrea were never found. Jackie's skull still had an ice pick lodged in it and Leah's skull showed multiple indentations from the blows of a hammer.

During the trial, the most damning evidence was the audiotape of the horrible torture that Lynette Ledford endured. Courtroom attendees were seen running from the courtroom in tears, visibly shaken by the vile recording. Deputy District Attorney Stephen Kay could barely speak to reporters without breaking into tears just after the playing of the tape. Many of the details from the transcription of that tape have been left out of this story simply because of the disgusting nature of it.

On March 18, 1980, Roy Norris pleaded guilty to all four counts of first-degree murder, second-degree murder (Andrea Joy Hall), two counts of rape, and one count of robbery. May 7th was his sentencing. Roy Norris was sentenced to forty-five years-to-life with parole eligibility in 2010. Norris decided not to attend his parole hearing in 2010 and has another parole eligibility in 2019.

On February 17, 1981, Lawrence Bittaker was found guilty

on all five murder counts and was sentenced to death. Due to California legal changes, Bittaker was never actually put to death and will most likely die in prison of old age. He's currently in San Quentin Prison and sometimes responds to letters from the public in which he signs with the nickname "pliers."

5

CHRIS COLEMAN

Chris Coleman grew up in an Evangelical Christian family in a small suburban town about an hour south of St. Louis, Missouri. His parents, Ron and Connie Coleman, were and still are co-pastors at the Grace Evangelical Church.

Shortly after high school, Chris joined the Marines and trained in the K9 unit as a dog handler. During his time in the military, he also worked in security, including a security detail for the US President.

Sheri Weiss grew up in Cicero, Illinois, just outside of Chicago and as a young girl was a White Sox fan. When she was ten, her family moved to Tampa Bay, Florida, where she played varsity softball and became a cheerleader. She and her best friend, Tara Lintz, graduated high school in 1995. After working briefly as a waitress, Sheri joined the Air Force and became an MP (Military Police).

Chris and Sheri met in Quantico, Virginia, while they were

both attending a dog training seminar and immediately hit it off. The couple started dating and not long after Sheri was unexpectedly pregnant. With Chris coming from such a religious background, it was clear the couple needed to get married.

Chris and Sheri, both still in their early twenties, eloped and got married in Chicago outside of his parents' church. Chris called his parents and told them the news, but they were clearly not thrilled. He had previously only introduced Sheri to them as a "friend from Chicago"; Sheri was not a born-again Christian and didn't fit into their Evangelical lifestyle.

A few months later, Sheri and Chris had their first son Garrett. Three years later his brother, Gavin, arrived in January 2000.

When Chris was just a small boy, his parents had become friends with a woman named Joyce Meyer. Joyce was also an Evangelical preacher who had worked her way up to become one of the most money-making preachers in the world.

Joyce preached what is known as "Prosperity Theology." It's a belief that insists that financial wealth is the will of God and that the more money you give to the church, God will look more favorably upon you and bring financial riches back to you.

Obviously, this type of belief comes with an ample amount of criticism. Especially when it comes from someone who flaunts wealth as much as Joyce Meyer.

To this day, Joyce is still one of the more successful Evangelical televangelists in the world. It's estimated that she makes well over $100 million per year traveling around the world in her $10 million personal jet preaching to huge crowds.

Her $20 million headquarters in Fenton, Missouri, are adorned with such extravagancies as a $23,000 antique marble toilet.

Chris' father, Ron, met with Joyce Meyer at a prayer conference and Joyce mentioned she needed someone to train a guard dog for her. Ron had the perfect candidate and reintroduced her to his son, Chris.

Chris trained Joyce's guard dog for her and managed to land himself a job on her security detail. It wasn't long thereafter that he was promoted to Chief of Security, a job that paid over $100,000 per year.

The job application came with a "spiritual requirement," meaning he had to be of the same faith, could not divorce, etc. Chris, of course, was well-versed in the evangelical movement and had even been "speaking in tongues" since 1996. By this time, Sheri had also become part of the evangelical movement. Eventually Sheri donated her time to Joyce's ministries in the world outreach program and also became an EMT.

With Chris' pay raise, the family moved to Columbia Lake, an affluent suburban family development situated on a small lake. It was a close-knit neighborhood where Sheri and the kids made friends with the nearby neighbors.

Though one wouldn't know it from the outside, things started turning bad for the couple in early 2008. Sheri had three friends that didn't know one another. If they had, things may have turned out differently.

In May of 2008, on Memorial Day, her neighbor Vanessa and her husband noticed that Sheri had bruises on her upper legs. Vanessa and her husband discussed whether thought it was abuse. They determined it wasn't and left well enough alone. Sheri normally wore long sleeves and pants, so they weren't sure if the bruises existed before that time or not.

Around the same time, Sheri confided in a different friend, Meegan, that Chris was beating her. Sheri sent Meegan a text, "Chris is gone right now, but he just beat me up. I'm ok though." Meegan and her husband pleaded with Sheri to come with them, but Sheri refused to leave Chris and go with them. Sheri insisted that Chris was sorry, and it wouldn't happen again.

Sheri's third friend was her best friend from high school, Tara Lintz. Tara was now divorced and living down in Tampa Bay, Florida, working as a cocktail waitress and jumping from boyfriend to boyfriend. In October of 2008, Sheri called Tara to tell her that Joyce Meyer was having a conference in Tampa Bay and that Tara should attend. By this time, Sheri had become quite religious and thought Tara's lifestyle was a bit reckless and she could be helped by Joyce's preaching.

Chris and Tara had already met when Tara visited them in Quantico, back before they were married. Sheri suggested she meet with Chris since he would be flying in a few days before the conference to make security preparations.

This, of course, was a mistake. Chris and Tara met for dinner and drinks and didn't waste any time in starting an affair. By the time the conference was over, Chris asked Joyce Meyer if he could spend a few extra days in Tampa Bay.

Immediately after Chris returned from Florida, he got on his laptop and created a document titled "All about Tara." He typed out her birthday, her dog's birthday, her height, weight, clothing sizes, favorite perfume, favorite sports teams, and even her favorite ice cream flavors. He even wrote down what their daughter's name would be; "Zoey Lynn Coleman." The heading of the document was "November 5, 2008. The day that Tara changed my life."

Almost immediately after Chris' arrival back home from Florida, he and Joyce received identical email threats. Four short emails sent within the span of five minutes.

Date: Fri 14 Nov, 2008 20:36:49

From: "Fuck Chris" <destroychris@gmail.com>

To: dmeyer@joycemeyer.org, joycemeyer@joycemeyer.org, davemeyer@joycemeyer.org, danmeyer@joycemeyer.org, davidmeyer@joycemeyer.org, ccoleman@joycemeyer.org

Subject: Fuck Chris's Family. They are dead!!!

Body: I'm sure this will make it to someone in the company. If you jackass's are like any other company this will be someone's account. Pass this on to Chris!! ! Tell Joyce to stop preaching the bullshit or Chris's family will die. If I can't get to Joyce then I will get to someone close to her and if I can't get to him then I will kill his wife and kids. I know Joyce's schedule so then I know Chris's schedule. If Joyce doesn't quit preaching the bullshit then they will die. During the Houston conference I will kill them all as they sleep. If I don't hit there then I will kill them during the book tour or the trip to India. I know where he lives and I know they are alone. Fuck them all and thy will die soon! Tell that motherfucker next time to let me talk to Joyce. She needs to hear what I have to say and now she will.

Date: Fri 14 Nov, 2008 20:38:51

From: "Fuck Chris" <destroychris@gmail.com>

To: ccoleman@joycemeyer.org

Subject: Go to Hell!

Body: Your family is done!

Date: Fri 14 Nov, 2008 20:39:37

From: "Fuck Chris" <destroychris@gmail.com>

To: ccoleman@joycemeyer.org

Subject: Houston Death?

Body: They will be done while you are gone at the Houston Conference. I know you will be out of town.

Date: Fri 14 Nov, 2008 20:42:11

From: "Fuck Chris" <destroychris@gmail.com>

To: ccoleman@joycemeyer.org

Subject: Houston Death

Body: Tell Chris his family is dead!! I know his schedule and they will die. Next time that motherfucker will let me talk to Joyce.

Chris immediately reported these threats to the local police. The police force in Columbia was small, but to be safe, they assigned extra patrols to drive by the Colemans' house daily.

Meanwhile, things at the Coleman household are getting worse. Chris has started to direct more hostility toward Sheri. On November 25, just a few days before Thanksgiving, Chris cornered Sheri in the kitchen to tell her he wanted a divorce. He told her that she and the boys were getting in the way of his career.

Sheri didn't want a divorce. She said she still loved him and asked her friends to pray for her and her marriage.

In mid-December, Chris had to take another business trip to Florida and met up with Tara once again in an Orlando hotel. This time they exchanged promise rings.

On December 21, Sheri called Chris and pled for him to come home for the holidays. He refused. He told her that she and the kids are keeping him from realizing God's destiny. He eventually came home on December 24.

The following week, on Jan 2, Chris called the local police. He had received another threat letter. This time the threat was typed on plain paper and was hand-delivered to their mailbox on his curb. Sheri was terrified.

The letter read:

> "Fuck You! Deny your God publically or else! No more oppurtunities. Time is running out for you and your family! Have a goodtime in India MOTHER FUCKER!"

Interestingly, both "publically" and "oppurtunities" were spelled incorrectly.

The city of Columbia was just a small town with a small police force and only two detectives. One of the detectives, Justin Barlow, just happened to live across the street from the Colemans and was assigned to the case.

Detective Barlow set up a camera from his own house facing the Colemans' house and mailbox, and also assigned extra patrols in the neighborhood.

That April, Chris had another trip with the Joyce Meyer Ministries. This time was to Maui, Hawaii, and of course he invited Tara.

Chris and Tara made sure that none of his co-workers spotted the two of them together. He knew that because of his job's "Spiritual Criteria Clause" he would lose his job if he was found to be having an affair.

During their time on Maui, Chris and Tara made more plans. Tara gave Chris a deadline on serving divorce papers to Sheri. She told him he had to serve them to her by May 4.

When Chris arrived back home from Maui and checked the mailbox on April 27, he found another threatening letter. The letter read:

> "Fuck you. I am giving you the last warning! You have not listened to me and you have not changed your ways. I have warned you to stop traveling and to stop carrying on with this fake religious life of stealing people's money. You think you are so special to do what you do protecting or think you are protecting her. She is a bitch and not worth you doing it. Stop today or else. I know your schedule! You can't hide from me ever. I'm always watching. I know when you leave in the morning and I know when you stay home. I saw you leave this morning. I will be watching. You better stop

traveling and doing what you are doing. THIS IS MY LAST WARNING! YOUR WORST NIGHTMARE IS ABOUT TO HAPPEN!"

Chris said his security camera caught someone putting the letter into the mailbox, but he didn't have a way of recording it. Strangely, Detective Barlow's camera across the street saw no activity around the mailbox.

When May 4th rolled around, Chris called Tara to tell her that his attorney said there were some typos on the divorce papers and he couldn't serve them to Sheri today, but he should be able to serve her the divorce papers the following day.

Of course, there was no attorney and there were no divorce papers.

That evening, Detective Barlow's camera, which was aimed at the Coleman mailbox, caught Chris, Gavin, and Garret playing baseball in the front yard just before sunset. The boys asked their father if they could stay the night at neighbor Brandon's house to celebrate his birthday, but Chris refused, telling them it's not a good night. This was a surprise to Brandon's mother, because they had been staying the night with him for the past several years on that specific night.

On the morning of May 5, 2009, just twelve hours after Chris was playing catch with his sons in the front yard, Detective Barlow got an early morning phone call that he would never forget. The time was 6:43 a m.

Chris was calling as he was driving home from the gym in St. Louis County to ask Detective Barlow to check on his house. Chris had been trying to contact Sheri by phone, but she wasn't answering. He said that Sheri and the kids should have been up by then and he was worried.

Detective Barlow called for backup, crossed the street, and knocked on the door. No answer. When his backup arrived just a few minutes later, they walked to the back of the house where they found a window to the basement wide open with the screen sitting next to the house.

The officers called for more backup and crawled through the window with guns drawn. As they climbed the stairs into the house, they were immediately hit with the smell of spray paint.

What they found as they entered the house was horrific. The scene looked like something that resembled the Manson murders.

The walls of the house were spray painted with rants similar to the letters and emails that Chris had been getting.

"U have paid"

"I saw you leave"

"Fuck you bitch punished"

"Fuck you I am always watching"

As they walked up the stairs to the second floor, Officer Donjon found thirty-one-year-old Sheri naked on her bed in the master bedroom with a black eye and ligature marks around her neck. He put his hand under her shoulder in an attempt to lift her and check if she was breathing, but rigor mortis had already set in and her body was stiff.

Officer Patton went into Gavin's room where he found the nine-year-old face down in his Spiderman pajamas. His skin was purplish and cold to the touch. Stiff. "Fuck you" was spray painted on the sheets covering him.

Detective Barlow went into eleven-year-old Garret's room. He too was cold and stiff. His lips were blue, his skin was grey, and he had ligature marks around his neck.

Though Chris was only seven minutes away when he called, it took him almost twenty minutes to arrive at the scene. The property was already strewn with cops and the house was surrounded with police tape.

When Chris arrived, he was told that his family was dead. He didn't attempt to go upstairs. He didn't ask how they died. He just sat on the driveway and sobbed. He then took out his Blackberry to call his work and his father.

When investigators brought Chris in for his statement, things immediately didn't seem to add up.

Chris claimed he left the house that morning to go to the gym at 5:43 a.m. and claimed his family was alive and well when he left. However, when the bodies were discovered just over an hour later, rigor mortis had already set in. Liver temperature was taken on the bodies and the forensic pathologist determined all three of them died sometime between 11 p.m. and 3 a.m.

During the interrogation, despite the interrogation room being very warm, Chris claimed to be very cold and asked for a blanket. When he was given a blanket Chris only covered his arms. That's when the Detectives noticed the scratches on his arms.

Investigators asked Chris how his relationship was with Sheri, and he admitted to having some communication problems but nothing that bad. They asked if there was anything going on in their relationship that Sheri would not have approved of and he mentioned that he texts Tara, "a ton." He insisted he wasn't having an affair, that Tara was just someone to talk to.

What Chris didn't know was that the investigators already knew about Tara. In fact, they had already spoken to the St. Petersburg Florida police who were already interrogating Tara at the same exact time. Tara was giving a different story of their relationship.

A Major Case Squad was assigned to the case with twenty-five investigators. The evidence started to pile up once investigators went through Chris' cell phone and computers.

On Chris and Tara's cell phones police found X-rated photos and videos the two of them had taken and sent back and forth to each other. There were sex videos of the two of them in Hawaii. In fact, Chris had even sent one of their sex videos to his own father, the Evangelical preacher. Their cell phones also revealed that Chris was texting Tara even while he was being held in the interrogation room.

When examining Chris' computer, they found the "All about Tara" document. However, more damning was a further analysis of his computer where the Forensics Team found evidence that the threatening emails came from Chris' own computer. Evidence of the typed letters was even recovered by the Forensics Team.

They additionally found that Chris commonly misspelled the

word "opportunities" in several other documents - misspelled the same way.

There was also the issue of Detective Barlow's camera. It was pointing at the house that entire night and caught no-one entering or leaving the house besides Chris.

When searching the house, investigators noticed that many of the windows had been left unlocked. It seems strange that someone who is the head of security for a large company and is getting personal death threats just days prior would leave windows open and unlocked.

Also in the house, they found a hardware store receipt for a can of red spray paint paid for by Chris.

Even the gym that Chris went to that morning was suspicious. The gym was unusually far away, and Chris had only been to that gym two times before. He joined the gym just a few days after he started the affair with Tara; it seems as if he had been planning the murders almost immediately after he started the affair.

Investigators traced the route between Chris' home and the gym. A latex glove stained with red spray paint and the faceplate from Chris' home security video recorder were found on the side of the road. They also found a piece of baling twine that had been tied into a noose. The Colemans had bales of hay in their back yard and one of the bales had a piece missing; the piece they found forensically matched that bale.

Though this seems like a massive amount of evidence, it was still largely circumstantial.

One wonders, why go through all of this trouble? Rather than killing your entire family, why would you not just get a divorce? The problem lies with Chris' job. Chris knew that, because of the clause for his job, if he was an adulterer or even got divorced he would most likely lose his high-paying job.

Chris Coleman was arrested on May 19, two weeks after the murders, and was charged with three counts of first-degree murder. He pled not guilty.

Despite previously having a $100,000 per year job, the judge determined that Chris was indigent (poor) and he was assigned two experienced death penalty defense attorneys.

Because of the nature of the murders, the media attention was massive and the public was outraged. So much so that Chris feared for his life and wore a bullet-proof vest when coming to trial.

Because of the media publicity, jurors were selected from Pickneyville, Illinois, over an hour away, and were bussed in every day. The trial began on April 25, 2011, almost two years after the murders.

During the trial, prosecutors introduced the X-rated pictures and videos. Tara showed up with bodyguards and while on the stand she wore the promise ring that Chris gave her.

The prosecution also called Joyce Meyer to testify that indeed, if it had been known that he was having an affair, it would have definitely jeopardized his job status.

Several of Sheri's friends testified that she had confided in them that Chris was beating her, wanted a divorce, and even that she knew Chris was having an affair with Tara.

However, the most critical piece of evidence was the time of death. Prosecutors showed the jury that Chris' story of the events didn't match the forensic evidence of the time of death.

Jurors began deliberations on May 4, 2011, and came back with a guilty verdict on all three counts. Chris Coleman was sentenced to life in prison without the possibility of parole.

To this day, Chris Coleman insists he is innocent. His parents still stand by him and he has unsuccessfully tried to appeal his conviction.

Tara was found to have no knowledge of Chris' plans.

6

DR. JOHN SCHNEEBERGER

Kipling, Saskatchewan, is a tiny Canadian farming town. If you blinked while you were driving on Highway 48, you might just miss it. With only about 1,000 residents, life is slow and pretty much everyone in town knows one another.

On Halloween night in 1992, a twenty-three-year-old single mother named Candice was finishing her shift at the only convenience store in the town. Candice had recently broken up with her boyfriend, Danny. Danny had stopped by to see her at work, but they got into a heated argument that escalated until Candice eventually got so upset that she sped off in her car. "I was so mad at Danny I felt like killing him."

Candice couldn't think straight and decided to drive to the Kipling Memorial Hospital to visit her friend that worked there.

She arrived to find that her friend wasn't working that night, but the nurses on duty could tell she was distraught and suggested she talk to the doctor.

Dr. John Schneeberger was the doctor working the night shift. Dr. Schneeberger had moved to Canada from South Africa and was a well-respected member of the small community, even helping the town get a public swimming pool built. The residents of Kipling considered themselves lucky to have such an educated and skilled doctor living in their tiny town.

Candice knew Dr. Schneeberger as well, as he had delivered her daughter earlier that year.

Candice told Dr. Schneeberger about her anxiety and he suggested a sedative and left the room. She was expecting him to offer a pill to calm her nerves, but she surprised to see him return to the examination room with a syringe.

Immediately after she received the shot, Candice recalls falling back on the table. "I fell over like a piece of jelly… I tried to scream as I fell over, but nothing would come out but a croaking noise."

Candice was partially unconscious, but still aware of what was going on. She could tell that someone was pulling down her jeans and laying her on her side facing the wall. Then she realized someone was inside her. Completely under the effect of the sedative, she could do nothing.

When Candice finally came to, she was too dizzy to drive home, so the nurses told her to stay the night in the hospital. The next morning when she awoke, she knew something was wrong and confronted Dr. Schneeberger. She asked what was that drug that he gave her, and his response was, "Why, did it give you crazy dreams?"

Candice knew she had been raped. She asked the nurses for an air-tight plastic bag and put her panties in it, then went home and immediately told her parents.

Since this was an extremely small town with only one hospital, the next morning Candice drove to Regina, a slightly larger town about ninety-five miles away to find a clinic that could perform a rape test.

In the Regina clinic, Candice gave samples from her panties, her jeans, and they took a vaginal swab to test for semen. The results of the test were positive. Candice then knew without a doubt that her suspicions were correct, and she had indeed been raped.

She also asked for her blood to be tested. The results of the blood test showed that she had a drug called Versed in her system. Versed is a pre-anesthetic used to induce anesthesia and is used for procedures like colonoscopies.

Candice went back to Kipling and filed a formal complaint with the Kipling Police Department. On November 2nd, Dr. Schneeberger volunteered to give a sample of his blood. He was adamant that he was innocent and that his blood DNA would not match the sample from Candice's rape kit.

Blood was taken from the doctor's arm and sure enough, he was correct. There was not a match.

After the DNA test was negative, Candice was still in disbelief. She spent the next year insisting to police that the DNA had been tampered with, but she had no way to prove it. Finally, after almost a year of pressure from Candice, in August 1993 Dr. Schneeberger agreed to a second voluntary DNA test.

This time the test was done by a Registered Nurse and the procedure was monitored by police. They watched the needle enter his arm, and the vials were taken directly to police headquarters.

Again, the second test did not match the DNA sample from Candice's panties. Candice was devastated.

After two failed DNA tests, residents of the small town of Kipling were not kind to Candice. Dr. Schneeberger was their hero; in such a small town he was a godsend. They considered themselves lucky to have such a skilled doctor in their tiny town, whereas Candice was just a high school educated single-mom. They rallied around the doctor and shunned Candice, believing that she was out for some sort of financial gain or that she had a romantic interest in the doctor but wanted to harm him because she was being rejected.

Residents were also suspicious of Candice because there were two nurses on shift the night of her alleged rape, but she said nothing to them.

After the second DNA test, and more ridicule from the townspeople, Candice moved from Kipling to the city of Red Deer, Alberta, nine hours away. The Royal Canadian Mounted Police closed the case in 1994 and Dr. Schneeberger continued with his practice and tried to get on with his life.

In 1995, Candice was still reeling with disbelief that the DNA tests didn't match. Out of ideas, she hired a private investigator named Larry O'Brien. O'Brien was a twenty-five-year veteran of the RCMP (Royal Canadian Mounted Police) who had done undercover and intelligence work in Southern Ontario. Candice tasked him with obtaining yet another DNA sample, but in a more covert manner.

On March 3, 1996 O'Brien broke into Dr. Schneeberger's car. Once inside his car, O'Brien collected a sample of hair from the headrest of the car. Unfortunately, there were no roots attached to the hair, so it had no useable DNA. He also found a lightly used tube of Chapstick Lip Balm in the ashtray. On the Chapstick would be epithelial cells that can be used for DNA testing. O'Brien took the Chapstick and rubbed it onto the plastic of a window envelope. He then bagged, timed, and initialed the sample and sent it to an independent forensic lab in British Columbia.

When the results came back, Candice was ecstatic. The DNA sample from the Chapstick matched the DNA from her panties. She was right all along.

Armed with this new DNA evidence, Candice returned to Kipling and demanded that the police re-open the case. Since this DNA sample was obtained without a warrant, the police couldn't use it as evidence. Also, there was no guarantee that the DNA from the Chapstick was actually Dr. Schneeberger's, so police did not reopen the case.

Police did however have their curiosities, but were apprehensive to officially charge him. Officers believed in the science of the DNA.

Candice was still completely baffled as to why the DNA from his arm did not match the DNA from the panties and lip balm, so she filed a Civil Suit against Dr. Schneeberger and brought charges against him with the medical society.

Again, with all the additional pressure, Dr. Schneeberger volunteered to have his blood taken a third time for another DNA test.

This time, to ensure the integrity of the test, the procedure was performed in the police forensics lab and recorded on video.

Not much blood is needed for a DNA test, so it's common

for a sample to be taken from a simple pinprick on the finger, but Dr. Schneeberger claimed he has a condition that causes him to bruise easily on his hands. He requested the sample be taken from his left arm. Since this was a voluntary test, and he was giving the sample in good faith, police complied with his request.

On Nov 20, 1996, police again videotaped the blood being drawn from Dr. Schneeberger's arm and the blood was taken inside a police lab. There were problems extracting the doctor's blood, however. Technician Jean Roney recalled, "The vein appeared larger than I would have expected, and I thought that was a little unusual."

Sometimes when extracting blood from a patient there, can be a bad vacuum in the vein which can cause the inability to get the blood out. Eventually she was able to get a sample of the blood, but she noticed something strange. "It's a little strange in that the blood doesn't look… really… fresh."

The lab attempted to test the blood anyway, but they eventually determined that it wasn't a large enough sample and the blood had been too degraded for an accurate DNA test.

Yet again, Candice was furious. "Oh my God that's bullshit! That's our last chance to get blood from him and you guys screwed up again?!"

However, just five months later, Candice would finally get a break, but that break would come at a great cost.

On the evening of April 25, 1997, just as police were about to ask for yet a fourth DNA test, Dr. Schneeberger's wife, Lisa, contacted police and accused her husband of raping her thirteen-year-old daughter, his stepdaughter.

The young girl had come to her mother with the information

and a condom wrapper that was left in her bed. The young girl said her step-father, Dr. Schneeberger, had been coming into her room in the middle of the night for years and inject her with something that would leave her with fleeting memories of sexual incidents with the doctor.

Lisa then searched her husband's home office and found a box with condoms, syringes, and drugs including Versed, and immediately called police.

Dr. Schneeberger was immediately arrested and ordered under a warrant to do a fourth DNA test. Since this test was no longer voluntary, the technician took three samples. The samples were taken from his hair, a saliva swab from his mouth, and a blood sample from his finger on his right hand - not the left arm where all three of the previous tests had been taken.

All three samples matched the DNA from the Chapstick and from the semen on Candice's panties.

Dr. John Schneeberger was officially charged with aggravated assault, which holds a maximum penalty of life in prison, two counts of administering a noxious substance to commit an indictable offense, which holds a maximum penalty of life in prison, one count of obstruction of justice, with a max penalty of ten years, and one count of sexual assault, with a max penalty of ten years.

It wasn't until the trial in November 1999 before the world found out how Dr. Schneeberger had thwarted police for seven years. The nurses and technician had seen the needle physically go into his arm each time, so how did the DNA come up different?

Dr. Schneeberger took the witness stand in his own defense and said that the first three times they drew blood, they were drawing someone else's blood. He had taken another of his male client's blood, inserted it into a thin rubber tube called a Penrose Drain along with an anti-coagulant to keep it in a liquid state, and implanted the tube into his own arm just next to his own vein. This was why he always insisted on having the blood taken from his left arm. In fact, during one of the videotapes, you can see that he wears a long sleeve shirt and does not pull it up far enough to see the incision in his upper arm and, for a split second, you can see the tube protruding from his arm.

This also explains why, on the third blood sample, the technician thought the blood looked dark and "not fresh." He had removed the tube from his arm after the second test, stored it in a refrigerator, then replaced it into his arm four years later for the third DNA test.

However, even after all of that, Dr. Schneeberger still claimed that none of what Candice said was true. His excuse was that he put the tube of blood into his arm because it was the only way to defend himself and he didn't trust the police. He claimed that Candice must have broken into his house and stolen a used condom from his trash in order to get the semen sample and frame him.

In reference to his defense, Judge Ellen Gunn said it was, "Inventive, fanciful, imaginative. However, one that does not apply is credible," and called his theory, "preposterous."

Of course, that defense was not near enough to convince a jury. He was convicted of two counts of sexual assault, one account of administering a noxious substance to commit an indictable offense, and one count of obstructing justice.

Amazingly, Dr. Schneeberger was sentenced to only six years in a minimum-security prison.

During Dr. Schneeberger's stay in prison, Lisa Schneeberger divorced him and fought with the legal system for the right to not allow him access to her daughters.

For Lisa Schneeberger, her agony was just getting started. When John was arrested, she had four children to support, one of which was only thirteen-months-old. She sold the house and car in order to pay the bills, filed for divorce, and took back her maiden name of Dillman.

On the evening before the guilty verdict was given, Lisa refused to let the girls sleep over with him as was required by the visitation agreement and she was ordered to pay a $2,000 fine for contempt of court.

While in jail, John insisted on visitation rights, but Lisa kept fighting. Despite her attempts to persuade judges and politicians, the court ordered her to force the girls to visit him once a month - a man that repeatedly drugged and raped their half-sister.

When the day finally came of the first forced visitation at the Bowden Institution where he was being held, about 100 protesters showed up at the gates to the prison and refused to let the car pass into the prison. The protesters were organized by Mad Mothers Against Pedophiles and claimed the courts are putting sex offenders' rights ahead of children's best interests. However, police eventually forced the crowds back and the car carrying the girls entered the prison. Upon entering the prison, the girls, age five and six, were scared to death, crying, and clinging to their mother's legs. A social worker eventually came to the rescue and called the visitation off.

The win, however, was short lived. Lisa eventually had to bring the girls to see their father on the last Sunday of every month. Eventually, after realizing the girls had no interest in visiting him, he dropped his visitation requests.

In 2002 Bob Mills, a member of Canadian Parliament lobbied for a bill called "Lisa's Law." It was an amendment to the Divorce Act to limit the rights of a child's access to sex offenders, but his bill did not pass.

During the following months, Lisa continued to fight her now ex-husband. She made sure the Canadian Immigration Department realized that he lied when he applied for citizenship by concealing information (his crimes) and making false representations.

Schneeberger served only four of his six-year sentence, much of it spent in Ferndale Prison in British Columbia, often referred to as "Club Fed." Ferndale is a minimum-security prison with residential-style housing, plenty of open spaces, and even a nine-hole golf course.

Schneeberger was stripped of his medical license and his Canadian citizenship and deported back to South Africa. He reportedly lives with his mother in Durban and works for a catering business.

7

MARY BELL

In the late 1960s, the Scotswood area of the town of Newcastle upon Tyne, England, was a rough area that was neglected and full of derelict houses and slums. The area was referred to as "Rat Alley." Many of the buildings were being torn down to make way for newer high-rise flats. However, despite its roughness and social problems, the community felt safe and children roamed unsupervised and commonly played in the broken-down homes.

One of the children that roamed the area was ten-year-old Mary Bell. Mary was a well-known bully in the area that the other children were clearly afraid of. Mary's teachers took note of her as well; though she was a smart and clever girl, she was better known for her sadistic side.

One of her teachers recalled Mary putting a cigarette out on another student's cheek simply because she got a better grade than her. Even though Mary admitted doing it, nothing was done to address her actions.

On Saturday May 11, 1968, Mary and her friend Norma Bell

(no relation) picked up a small boy age three and told him they were taking him to buy candy. The little boy was found later dazed and bleeding and wandering the streets. The police were called, but again, no action was taken.

The very next day, the Newcastle Police received a complaint from a mother that Mary had tried to strangle her daughter in a playground while Norma held the girl down. Yet again, this is a complaint against a ten-year-old girl, so nothing was done by the police.

On May 25, the day before Mary's 11th birthday, Mary found four-year-old Martin Brown playing outside with his friends. She told the boy she wanted to play a game with him and took him to one of the nearby derelict houses. She took Martin upstairs and told him that he had a sore throat and she could make it better by massaging his neck. Mary placed her hands around his throat and strangled the life out the boy.

A few hours later, a construction worker found the boy's lifeless body in the building and called for help. A neighbor contacted Martin's mother who ran to the home to find him pale and lifeless with no marks on him, just a trickle of blood coming from the corner of his mouth.

When police investigated the death, they noticed there were some pills lying around the upstairs of the house. Initially, they thought that may have been the cause of death, but later it was ruled out and considered a "natural death." They thought the boy may have "died of fright" because he had previously fallen down a flight of stairs.

The local newspapers referred to Martin Brown as the "Rat Alley Boy."

In the days following Martin's death, Mary showed up at his

mother's door. "I've come to see Martin," she said to his mother. Martin's mother, assuming she didn't know Martin had died, told her that Martin was dead. Mary said "Oh, I know he's dead, I want to see him in his coffin." Martin's mother was shocked and slammed the door.

As the days went by, Mary actually told family members and other kids at school that she had killed Martin Brown, but nobody believed her. In her school notebook she drew a picture of Martin's body the way it was lying in the house and a bottle of pills next to his body. Next to the pills was the word, "tablet" and also a workman finding the body.

She also wrote in the notebook, "There were crowds of people beside an old house. I asked what was the matter, there has been a boy who just lay down and died." All of this went completely unnoticed by authorities until much later.

Two days after Martin's death there was a break-in at a nursery. Police found four pieces of paper with scribbles that said, "I murder so that I may come back." Another said, "We murder, watch out." Yet another said, "We did murder Martin Brown. Fuck off you bitch." Police, however, dismissed these notes as a childish prank.

Martin's death was blamed on the "Rat Alley Slums" and there were protesters that marched down the streets claiming that the clearance of the old buildings wasn't being done properly. Mary Bell participated in the protests on July 31st.

Mary's home life was not like other children. Mary's mother, Betty Bell, was a well-known prostitute in the area with a specialty in bondage and sadomasochism. Betty would bring her clients home where Mary would witness the BDSM acts and, at the age of four, Mary was forced to engage in sex acts with her clients.

Betty had made repeated attempts to kill Mary within her first few years of life, giving her pills as sweets then later claiming she accidentally took her sleeping pills. Other family members became suspicious when Betty claimed Mary had fallen from a window. Betty made other attempts to give Mary away to relatives, then later changing her mind and taking her back.

Betty was well-known for going away for weeks on end, leaving Mary alone and unsupervised. Mary's father, Billy, was no better. Billy was rarely there and, when he was, he was drunk and physically abusive to both Betty and Mary.

It's no wonder Mary turned out the way she did.

Two months after Martin's death, Mary struck again, this time with her friend Norma.

The public at this time still had no idea there was a killer amongst them. They thought Martin's death was the fault of the development companies. Children still played unsupervised in the streets, even at the youngest of ages.

Four-year-old Brian Howe was playing by himself, watching the demolition of the houses of Rat Alley when Mary and Norma approached him and took him to an area referred to as the "Tin Lizzy," a small wasteland.

When Brian was reported missing a few hours later, police found him half naked, in a spread-eagle position with a pair of scissors and a lock of his hair found near his body. Police found that he had been strangled, cut on the legs, punctures on the calves, and cuts on his penis in an attempt to cut it off. There was also a letter cut into his stomach, "M," almost as if she wanted to get caught. Exams determined that the cuts were inflicted after death.

Still, at this point, nobody connected the two deaths. Days later, as Brian's coffin was carried out of his home, a police officer noticed Mary, smiling.

When investigators realized that the cuts on Brian's stomach was an initial, they then knew they were looking for a child and they now assumed that the two murders were linked.

Police announced in a press conference that they were looking for a child and Mary seemed to want to draw attention to herself. She was listening intently, right at the front of the press conference.

Because Mary had previously bragged about Martin's killing, word got around to police and they started to look into Mary.

Speaking to Mary's father Billy, Mr. Bell initially refused to let police speak to her, but she was eventually brought in for questioning.

Police had by that time spoken to a nine-year-old boy who had witnessed the strangling of Brian Howe. Mary denied the killing and said, "Send for my solicitor!"

The community initially felt sorry for Mary, assuming at only ten years old that she had no idea what she had done.

Despite Mary's denials, the evidence piled up. Police made the connection between Mary and the notes that were found two months earlier.

Speaking to her teachers, police found her school notebook where she had drawn a picture of Martin Brown's body with the word "tablet" next to the body. The information about the tablets (pills) found near the body had not been released to the public; they knew then that Mary was the killer.

Mary's friend Norma, when questioned, admitted the murder, but claimed it was all Mary.

> "Mary Bell was standing in front of the Howe's house when the coffin was brought out. I was, of course, watching her. And it was when I saw her there that I knew I did not dare risk another day. She stood there, laughing. Laughing and rubbing her hands. I thought, My God, I've got to bring her in, she'll do another one."
>
> - Detective Chief Inspector James Dobson, Newcastle Police

On Aug 8, 1968 Mary was charged with murder.

Detectives were stunned by Mary's intelligence level. She was clearly cunning despite her age, denying accusations and seemingly anticipating the questions before they were asked.

The local police were as disturbed as anyone over the arrests. They had never encountered offenders of such a young age.

During the trial, Mary was nonchalant, as if she had no idea what she was accused of. Dancing near her seat and turning around during proceedings asking for candy.

Normally in England, the accused will sit alone in a box. However, because of the extraordinary circumstance of having such a young defendant, the judge allowed the lawyers to sit with their client.

The trial lasted nine days in which Mary and Norma were allowed to state their case. The Prosecutor, Rudolph Lyons, started the proceedings by linking the two murders, suggesting that Brian and Martin's murders were done by the same people.

Handwriting experts were brought in to analyze the confessional notes found in the nursery and the drawings from Mary's school notebooks. The jury was then told of how Mary and Norma morbidly taunted the victim's families by asking to see bodies.

Forensic evidence was also presented in the form of gray fibers from Mary's wool dress that was discovered on the bodies of both victims. Maroon fibers from Norma's skirt were also found around Brian's shoes. The prosecution presented a strong case against both girls.

As the trial moved along, it became clear that Mary was a dominant figure between the two girls and Norma was simply a follower. Norma was clearly overwhelmed by the trial and observers took pity upon her, while Mary would give quick and witty remarks as if she hadn't a care in the world.

Prosecutors also called on psychiatrists who examined Mary and testified that she suffered from psychopathic personality disorder, demonstrated a lack of empathy, and was liable to act on impulse.

The jury deliberated for five hours and returned with their verdict. Norma was considered "simple minded" and was acquitted of the charge of manslaughter. Mary was found not guilty of murder, but found guilty of manslaughter and was sentenced to lifetime detention.

The jury and trial observers heard nothing of Mary's home life and how that may have affected her actions.

Because of Mary's young age, authorities wanted to attempt

to rehabilitate her rather than punish her, believing that Mary didn't truly understand what she had done.

She was too young to go to a mental hospital, so Mary was assigned to a secure school where she could be given constant attention.

The people of Newcastle agreed and felt sympathy for Mary because of her young age and upbringing, despite her horrible crimes.

Mary spent twelve years in detention. She spent six years in Red Bank Juvenile Institution where she was the only girl with twenty-two boys. During her time there, she continued to blame others for her crimes, never admitting her own offenses.

Mary's mother Betty visited her in school, but Mary eventually blamed her for the crimes, writing her the following letter:

> "Please Mam, put my tiny mind at ease, tell judge and jury on your knees. They will listen to your cry of 'please'. The guilty one is you, not me. I am sorry it has to be this way. We'll both cry and you will go away. Tell them you are guilty, please. So then Mam, I'll be free. Your daughter, May."

Betty Bell gave a TV interview years later, clearly broken and suffering from drug and alcohol addiction.

In 1980, at the age of twenty-three, Mary was released and given a new identity. She had a daughter while she was in captivity and the media eventually tracked the daughter down, who knew nothing of Mary's crimes until she was told. In 2003, Mary and her daughter won a case in the high court which then gave them both anonymity for life.

8

MICHELLE BICA

Michelle and Thomas Bica were ecstatic to find out that Michelle, thirty-nine, was pregnant again. The couple had been trying to conceive again ever since the miscarriage that Michelle had the prior year.

The couple attended birthing classes, showed friends their sonogram photos, and Michelle shopped for maternity clothes. Thomas had even prepared a nursery for the baby. As time went by, the pregnancy seemed to be coming along normally with the exception of the due date, which occasionally got pushed further and further out.

In September 2000, Michelle and Thomas were shopping at Walmart where they met Jon and Theresa Andrews. The Andrews' were also expecting a baby, and both couples were shopping for baby supplies. The two couples discussed their due dates, genders of their babies, and baby-related chit chat when they discovered they were neighbors that lived only four blocks away from each other.

Jon and Theresa Andrews had been high school sweethearts. In 1996, the couple were married and four years into their marriage they decided it was time to start a family.

Just a few days after the chance meeting of the two couples, Michelle announced that she got a call from her doctor. She said the doctor had told her that the original sonogram had been a mistake and her baby was actually going to be a boy rather than a girl.

On the morning of September 27, 2000 Jon Andrews was at work when he received a call from Theresa. The couple had been trying to sell their Jeep Wrangler and Theresa was going out to meet a woman that was interested in buying it. Jon called her a few hours later to find out if she sold it but Theresa didn't pick up.

When Jon got home from work, he found both Theresa and the Jeep were gone, but her handbag and cell phone were still in the house. Jon immediately knew something was wrong as Theresa wouldn't leave without those.

While Jon was going through panic over his missing wife, just four blocks away the Bica household was overjoyed.

Thomas Bica got a call from his wife while he was at work. Michelle announced that her water broke, and she was rushed to the hospital by ambulance where she gave birth to a beautiful baby boy. However, rather than keep her there, she and the baby were immediately sent home because of a tuberculosis scare at the hospital.

The Bicas named their newborn Michael Thomas Bica. Friends and family came to visit the couple and see the new baby boy. While Thomas was an excited new father, Michelle seemed stressed and upset. She told Thomas that she was very upset to hear the news of the disappearance of Theresa Andrews and, out of respect, she didn't want to put the "New Baby" flag in the front yard as they had planned.

Meanwhile, at the Andrews house, friends and family were desperately searching for clues to the disappearance of Theresa. The following week police detectives get their first clue when they trace Theresa's cell phone records. They find that the call that Theresa got about the Jeep they had for sale actually came from Michelle Bica's phone.

Police immediately questioned Michelle Bica and her husband Thomas. Michelle appeared combative and agitated. The FBI checked out her story of the birth and found that the hospital had no record of her and there had not been any tuberculosis scare; her story was clearly a lie.

When detectives returned to Michelle's house to question her further, she quickly disappeared into the bedroom, put a handgun into her mouth, and pulled the trigger. Detectives found Thomas outside of the locked bedroom crying.

Child services immediately took the newborn to the hospital where DNA tests were performed that proved that Jon Andrews was actually the baby's father.

Thomas Bica was taken into custody and questioned. He explained that he had believed everything that Michelle had told him about the pregnancy. After twelve hours of poly-graph examinations, police determined that Thomas had no idea that his wife had faked her pregnancy, and he was released.

Upon searching the Bica house, police found a shallow grave in the garage covered with gravel. Inside was the body of Theresa Andrews - she had a gunshot wound in her back and her womb was cut open in a makeshift cesarean where Michelle had removed the baby.

Amazingly, the baby survived and was returned to Jon Andrews.

9

BONUS CHAPTER: THE GIRL IN THE BARREL

This chapter is a free bonus chapter from True Crime Case
Histories: Volume 2
http://truecrimecasehistories.com/book2/

On September 2, 1999 in the suburban town of Jericho,
New York, just thirty miles from Midtown Manhattan, Ronald Cohen was preparing to sell his house. He had
just found a buyer for the property at $455,000 and the new
owner wanted to take a final walk-through before taking
ownership.

The buyer was very thorough and, during the walk-through,
wanted to see the crawlspace beneath an addition that had
been built onto the back of the house about thirty years
before.

The crawlspace was only thirty-six inches high so the two
men had to hunch down to get through the large space. At
the very back of the crawlspace they noticed a fifty-five-

gallon barrel on its side, wedged beneath the stairs. The buyer asked Mr. Cohen about the barrel and he said it had been there since he bought the property over ten years before. He had no idea what was in it or how it got there. It was far too heavy to move by himself so he had just left it there since he never used the crawlspace anyway. The buyer said he wanted it removed before he would purchase the property. Mr. Cohen and his real estate agent got some help and rolled the barrel out from underneath the home and took it to the curb for the trash workers to haul away.

When sanitation workers showed up the next day, they informed Mr. Cohen that, at 355 pounds, the barrel was far too heavy for them to take away and since they had no idea what it contained, it would need to be emptied to make sure there was nothing hazardous or toxic inside.

Mr. Cohen and his real estate agent decided to open the barrel and separate whatever was inside so it could be disposed of properly. There was a metal seal around the top of the barrel, so with some tools, they pried the barrel open. The two men were immediately hit with an overwhelming stench. The unmistakable stench of death.

Once the lid was removed they could see a curled human hand and a woman's shoe. The barrel was filled with a green viscous fluid surrounded by tiny plastic pellets. Mr. Cohen immediately called police.

Police took the barrel to the forensics lab where they emptied it onto a large white tarp so they could collect any evidence. Inside the barrel they found a small mummified female body. The body had been crumpled over and bent in half to fit into the barrel. Because the barrel was sealed so tightly, her body had been fairly well preserved, with skin the consistency of rubber, but when it hit the air it began decaying quickly and was immediately taken away for an autopsy.

During the autopsy they determined that the body was that of a female of Hispanic descent. She was tiny, only about four foot nine inches tall, with long black hair, and some unusual gold bridgework on her teeth. The bridgework was not something commonly done in the United States at the time and had most likely been done in South America somewhere. The cause of death was determined to be blunt-force trauma to the head. Someone had used a hammer of some sort to smash her head seven to ten times, crushing her skull. She was also eight to nine months pregnant. Police collected DNA from the fetus to see if they could later match it to a father.

When police emptied the rest of the barrel, it oozed out a strange, green, gooey liquid, possibly a chemical dye of some sort. They also noticed tiny black-and-white plastic pellets mixed in the goo. The woman's clothes were still intact and seemed to be a style from the Sixties. Near the bottom of the barrel they found a woman's purse with some cosmetic items inside and a badly damaged address book. There was also a green stem from a plastic flower arrangement.

At the bottom of the barrel were three pieces of jewelry: two gold rings, one of them with an inscription reading "M.H.R. XII 59"; and a locket that was engraved, "To Patrice Love Uncle Phil."

The pages of the address book were badly damaged and stuck together with the green goo. Detectives weren't hopeful of getting any clues from it, but just in case, it was put inside a forensic drying cabinet for a few days to dry out.

The following day, detectives began researching to find out

where the barrel may have come from. The homeowner, Mr. Cohen, explained that it was already there when he bought the house several years earlier. Detectives began going back through the prior owners to find out who built the extension on the house.

After researching four prior owners, they eventually found the homeowner who built the extension on the home. He was now seventy-one years old and lived in Boca Raton, Florida. His name was Howard Elkins. He sold the house back in 1972 and retired when he closed his plastics business that he owned in Manhattan. Police wanted to question him, but they wanted to collect more information before making the trip south.

As the days went by, the clues started to pour in. On the side of the barrel were the printed letters "GAF," which turned out to be a chemical company based in New Jersey. Police took photos of the barrel and brought some of the pellets and a sample of the green dye to them for analysis. GAF confirmed that the pellets were polyethylene pellets that were used to make many plastic products; one of these products was plastic flowers. The green dye was a unique product called Halogen Green, which was a dye specifically used to make plastic flower bases in the 1960s. The only customer they had for that product was a company called Melrose Plastics. It was the same company that Howard Elkins had closed in 1972.

Meanwhile, the forensic documents lab made some progress on the damaged address book. They were able to get it dried enough to where they could get the pages separated, but the ink had completely disintegrated from the pages. Using a device called a video spectral comparator they were able to read some of the information on the documents by using alternative light sources. The first notation in the book was a number that started with the letter "A." It was a resident alien number. Detectives spoke with immigration officers, but the number was from thirty years ago and their systems had changed since then. It would take time for them to come back with a result.

Knowing that the barrel, the plastic, and the dye all came from Howard Elkins' business, and they'd found the barrel beneath Elkins' former home, detectives now believed they had enough information to take a trip to Florida and question him. But before questioning him they wanted to visit his former business partner in the plastic flower business, Melvin Gantman, who had also since retired to Boca Raton.

Mr. Gantman confirmed that he and Mr. Elkins were business partners, but he hadn't spoken to him in years. When shown a photo of the barrel, Gantman quickly confirmed that the barrel was one that they often used for their company. He also verified the dye color and plastic pellets were what they used in making their plastic flowers. When shown a photo of the plastic stem found in the barrel, he knew that it was from their company as well.

The most useful information Gantman gave, however, was something he recalled from back in the late Sixties. He knew that Elkins was having an affair with a Hispanic employee at the company and had rented an apartment for her. He didn't know her name, but he remembered that she had strange gold teeth in the front and long black hair. Gantman recalled getting a phone call from the landlord of the apartment Elkins was renting for her. The landlord was looking for Elkins. The apartment was now empty, but the belongings were still in the apartment and the landlord wanted him to get the things moved out so it could be rented again.

Detectives were now more convinced than ever that seventy-one-year-old Elkins was the killer. They went to his home and Elkins invited them in. All the things that Gantman easily remembered from the business, Elkins didn't seem to recall at all. He had no recollection of the barrel, the dye, or the plastic pellets. Nothing.

Surprisingly, when asked if he'd had an affair during that time he freely admitted that he had. All he could say was "Yes, a very short affair. She left." When asked if he knew she was pregnant or even if he knew her name, he seemed to not remember anything about her.

Detectives informed him that the girl was found pregnant and deceased in a barrel beneath his former house. He seemed completely unfazed. When they asked him for a sample of his DNA, he flatly refused.

Just then his phone rang. It was his wife. After speaking briefly to his wife, Elkins told the detectives that they needed to leave. He said his wife was coming home and that the two of them would have a lot to talk about.

The New York detectives had no jurisdiction in Florida to get a warrant or make an arrest. Before they left, they informed Elkins that they would be back with a warrant and put him in jail for the rest of his life.

Early the following morning the two detectives received a call from the local Palm Beach Police Department. Elkins was nowhere to be found and his wife had put in a missing persons report.

Friends, family, and the police were all searching for Howard Elkins. He was found later that evening in his neighbors' garage in the back seat of their Ford Explorer SUV. That morning he had gone to Walmart and purchased a 12-gauge

Mossberg shotgun. Elkins sat in the back seat of the SUV, put the shotgun between his legs and the barrel in his mouth, and shot himself in the head.

Not that there was any question of his guilt, but detectives now collected his DNA from the scene and took it back to New York where it was confirmed that he was the father of the fetus.

As soon as they returned to New York, eight days after the barrel was found, they got word back from Immigration with the identity of the victim. Her name was Reyna Angelica Marroquin, and she had immigrated to the U.S. in 1966 from El Salvador.

The forensic document team was also able to get much more information from the address book. They recovered several names, addresses, and phone numbers. The phone numbers were over thirty years old, so detectives didn't have much hope for them, but they tried calling anyway. Amazingly, one phone number still worked. The woman that answered, Kathy Andrade, was a close friend of Reyna and was still living at the same location three decades later.

Kathy identified Reyna from a thirty-year-old immigration photo. She said Reyna immigrated from El Salvador and worked making plastic flowers at Melrose Plastics in the Sixties.

In November 1968 Reyna had told Kathy that she had been dating her boss at the flower factory and was pregnant with his baby. Kathy didn't know his name, only that it was Reyna's boss at the flower factory. One day Reyna told her that she had made a terrible mistake. She said she'd gotten mad at him and called his wife. Reyna told his wife that her husband was having an affair with her, had promised to marry her, and that she was pregnant with his baby. Reyna told Kathy she was terrified that he would kill her. It turns out her assumption was right. That was the last time that Kathy ever heard from Reyna.

Kathy recalled going to Reyna's apartment one evening and there were two plates set out for dinner. Dinner was still warm on the stove, but there was no sign of Reyna. She called police at the time to report her as missing, but was told that if she wasn't a family member she couldn't file a missing persons report. She tried to call Reyna every day for weeks after that, but never heard from her and eventually gave up.

Oscar Corral, a journalist covering the story for *Newsday*, a daily newspaper in the New York City area, later tracked down Reyna's ninety-five-year-old mother in San Salvador, El Salvador, and flew down to visit her. Her mother said she would speak to Reyna regularly on the phone, then suddenly the contact stopped and she had no idea why. She said she would often dream of Reyna trapped inside a barrel.

Reyna's body was transported back to El Salvador to be buried. Her mother died one month later and was buried next to her.

Thank you for reading this bonus chapter. Please check out the rest of True Crime Case Histories: Volume 2 on Amazon.

http://truecrimecasehistories.com/book2/

10

BONUS CHAPTER: THE COFFEE KILLER

This chapter is a free bonus chapter from True Crime Case
Histories: Volume 3
http://truecrimecasehistories.com/book3/

Nestled beneath the Harbor Bridge in Sydney, Australia, was the Billy Blue College of Design. Sydney was a long way from Indonesia, which was perhaps why Mirna Salihin and Jessica Wongso became such close friends. They had both started their first year at the prestigious school for graphic design, and they had both come from Jakarta, Indonesia, specifically to attend this school.

The young girls were like two peas in a pod. Both girls came from wealthy Indonesian families, and both had a passion for graphic design and were eager to start their careers. The two young girls were inseparable.

After graduation from college, however, Mirna went back to Jakarta to work where her family still lived, while Jessica stayed in Sydney. Jessica loved Sydney so much that her parents and two siblings also immigrated there in 2008.

Jessica Wongso & Mirna Salihin

As the years went by, Jessica and Mirna kept in touch. Both had secured well-paying jobs doing graphic design, and both had fallen in love with young men. Mirna, with a young Indonesian man and Jessica with a young Australian man, but the men differed greatly from each other.

In 2014, when Mirna took a vacation back to Sydney, the two girls met to catch up. During their time together, Mirna and Jessica discussed their lives, their work, and their boyfriends. During the discussion of boyfriends, Mirna was surprised to learn that Jessica's boyfriend, Patrick O'Connor, was a bit of a bad boy. When the girls were friends at college, they were pretty conservative, concentrating on their studies, but now Jessica was dating a guy with a completely different way of life. O'Connor was involved in drugs and alcohol, and his habits seemed to be rubbing off on Jessica.

Despite their solid friendship for so many years, the two girls argued about Jessica's boyfriend. It was clear that Mirna didn't approve of her dating a man that was such a bad influence on her and told her in no uncertain terms that she should get away from him. Mirna told her that this guy was messing up her future, and if she didn't change her path, it would change her life forever.

Jessica didn't take this advice well and told Mirna that she loved Patrick despite his faults and would stick with him. She became furious with Mirna to the point where Mirna was uncomfortable being alone with her. The rest of her Sydney trip became awkward, and Mirna made sure that there was always another friend with them whenever they went out.

But despite her initial objections, Jessica reluctantly took Mirna's advice and dumped her druggie boyfriend. But because of this, she secretly harbored deep resentment toward Mirna for suggesting that she leave the man she loved. Leaving him didn't stop her problems, though. They were only getting started.

After breaking up with Patrick, Jessica developed a drinking problem, and her attitude towards friends and co-workers began to change. Over the next two years, Jessica drank more and more until one night in August 2015 while driving drunk, she plowed her car over a curb, across a grassy area, and through the wall of a busy nursing home. Her car landed within meters of the bedrooms of elderly residents. The fiasco landed her a DUI, a cracked rib, some time in jail, and an embarrassing video of her on the nightly news. Despite potentially killing residents of the nursing home, Jessica was angry rather than apologetic.

Throughout 2014 and 2015, Jessica attempted suicide five times. She was admitted to Royal Prince Alfred Hospital each time, and when she returned to work, she told her boss,

> "Those bastards in the hospital didn't allow me to go home, and they treated me like a murderer. If I want to kill someone, I know exactly the right dose."

In October 2015, during one of her failed suicide attempts, Jessica had tried to poison herself. Police found her unconscious with a bottle of whiskey and three handwritten letters next to her bed. One letter blamed her ex-boyfriend, Patrick O'Connor, for her death. She addressed two other letters to her family and work friends, saying her goodbyes.

Jessica's anger and alcohol problems were affecting her work. She worked as a graphic designer at a firm called New South Wales Ambulance, but despite working there less than a year, she developed deep-seated anger toward her boss, Kristie Carter. At one point, Jessica threatened Kristie because she wouldn't help Jessica to find a place to stay after crashing her car into the nursing home, "You must die, and your mother must die." Kristie reported the threat to the local police.

Jessica now regretted her break-up with Patrick. During this time, she sent him countless text messages and voicemails. She threatened to hurt herself, hurt him, and hurt his friends if he didn't take her back. Patrick wanted nothing to do with her. She was clearly unstable, and in December 2015, Australian Police issued an urgent restraining order against her.

Back in Jakarta, Mirna was having the time of her life. Her picture-perfect life was that of a wealthy socialite. She had a well-paid job that she loved and was planning her dream wedding. But because of Jessica's continuing problems and their uncomfortable discussion, Mirna decided not to invite her to her wedding.

In her mind, Jessica already thought Mirna was to blame for all of her problems. Her downward spiral was all a result of Mirna's advice. So, her anger and resentment escalated when she wasn't invited to Mirna's wedding.

Mirna and Arief Soemarko had an island wedding in Bali in late 2015. The wedding ceremony was elaborate and straight out of a fairy tale. They had plans to honeymoon in Korea and wanted to start a family as soon as they could.

Just a few days after the wedding, Jessica continued her downward spiral and was fired from her graphic design job at New South Wales Ambulance. Now jobless, Jessica took some time to come back to Jakarta, Indonesia, to visit friends. She wanted to get together with Mirna to let her know there were no hard feelings, and she wanted to congratulate her on her wedding.

The two girls agreed to meet for coffee at 5:15 p.m. on January 6, 2016 but Mirna was apprehensive, despite Jessica's assurance of good intentions. Mirna wanted someone to accompany her, so she asked their mutual friend, Hani, to go with her. Hani had also attended Billy Blue College with them in Sydney.

Jessica arrived oddly early at Olivier, a trendy restaurant in the posh Grand Indonesia Shopping Mall in central Jakarta. Mirna thought it was unusual when Jessica texted her at 1 p.m., insisting she would pre-order the coffee for the three girls. Mirna assured her there was no need for that and that she would order when they arrived later that afternoon.

Jessica arrived at Olivier at 3:30 p.m., more than ninety minutes before Mirna and Hani were scheduled to arrive. She walked around the restaurant, looking for the perfect table, then left the restaurant to do some shopping. She wanted to buy some gifts for her friends, so she stopped into Bath & Body Works. Jessica purchased three small bottles of bath soap for the three of them and arrived back at Olivier at 4:14 p.m. with three large gift bags. The gift bags were unusually large for only having a single small bottle of bath soap in them.

Security cameras showed Jessica walking around the entire restaurant, looking for the perfect table, occasionally glancing directly at the cameras. After a few minutes of searching, she chose a half-circle booth on the side of the restaurant with large palm trees behind it. The palm trees behind the booth conveniently obscured the security camera behind them, leaving only a single security camera across the restaurant pointing directly at the table.

Jessica then placed the large gift bags on the table, waited a few moments, then moved the bags more toward the center of the table. Almost an hour before Mirna and Hani were due to arrive at the restaurant, Jessica ordered a Vietnamese iced coffee for Mirna and two additional coffee drinks for herself and Hani. When the drinks arrived at 4:24 p.m., Jessica was seen on the security camera doing something with the drinks, but the cameras didn't pick up the details because of the gift bags that were blocking the view.

The drinks then sat on the table for fifty-two minutes until Mirna and Hani arrived at 5:16 p.m. Within a few seconds of sitting down, Mirna took a big drink of the Vietnamese iced coffee that Jessica had ordered for her and immediately knew something was wrong. She began rapidly waving her arm in front of her mouth and told the girls that there was something wrong with the coffee. She pushed the glass away from her and continued frantically waving her hand. In less than sixty seconds, Mirna's head fell back against the top of the padded booth. Her eyes rolled back in her head, her body began to convulse violently, and she started foaming from her mouth.

Restaurant staff and other patrons of the restaurant started to gather around. Their first assumption was that Mirna was an epileptic, and she was having a seizure. Hani was crying and panicking and called Mirna's husband. Jessica, however, showed no signs of stress at all.

Mirna was unresponsive, and emergency medical workers carried her out of the restaurant in a wheelchair, rushing her to the hospital, but she died shortly afterwards.

Jessica was the first person to make accusations. When people had started gathering around at the restaurant, Jessica immediately said to the restaurant manager, Devi Siagian, "What did you put inside the drinks?!" Because of this accusation, Devi had the foresight to collect the three coffee glasses and saved them in the back of the restaurant until the police arrived.

In the days after her death, it was assumed that Mirna had died of an epileptic seizure, and Jessica and Hani were not questioned at the scene. It wasn't until three days after Mirna's death when police analyzed the contents of the Vietnamese iced coffee that they realized she didn't die of an epileptic seizure. Mirna's drink contained a lethal dose of cyanide, and the case was now considered a homicide.

Mirna's family initially objected to an autopsy. Indonesia is a predominantly Muslim country, and it was not common for autopsies to be conducted as it mutilates the body, but the police assured the process would be brief. Mirna's family agreed to an autopsy, and on January 10, the medical examiner found that there was bleeding in Mirna's stomach, consistent with that of a corrosive substance. Traces of cyanide were found in her stomach but not in any of her other internal organs.

When police analyzed the security camera footage from the restaurant, Jessica was seen awkwardly backing away from the scene while Mirna was convulsing. She was doing something odd with her hands, but it's unclear exactly what she was doing. Speculation was that she was moving something from one hand to the other, while another theory was that she was scratching her finger because she had just stirred poison into Mirna's drink using her finger.

(A link to the security camera footage can be found in the online appendix at the end of this book.)

When the Grand Indonesian Police heard about the relationship problems between Jessica and Mirna, they turned to the authorities in Sydney to look into Jessica's background. They had abolished the death penalty in Australia since the 1980s, but it was still in effect in Indonesia and was carried out by firing squad. The Australian Federal Police only agreed to help investigate the case after assurances from the Indonesian government that prosecutors would not seek the death penalty.

The Australian Federal Police shared the confidential history of Jessica's troubles; her DUI charges, her multiple suicide attempts, her death threat to her former boss, and the restraining order her ex-boyfriend had issued against her.

They also interviewed her former boss, Kristie Carter, for nine hours. Later, Kristie's testimony became key evidence in the case against Jessica.

Within weeks, Indonesian Police officially charged Jessica with the murder of Mirna Salihin. Dressed in an orange prison jumpsuit and a sign hanging around her neck with her name on it, police took Jessica back to the Olivier restaurant for a reenactment of the crime.

Indonesian news outlets and social media quickly became obsessed with the case, and Jessica was thrust into the public spotlight. Reporters and cameras followed Jessica's every step, and she strangely seemed to enjoy the attention. Television cameras showed Jessica smiling and waving as if she was unaware of the reason for all the attention.

Despite the agreement between the Australian Federal Police and the Grand Indonesian Police, prosecutors said the agreement not to seek the death penalty would be void if they convicted her on evidence the Jakarta police had gathered. The Indonesian police also argued that Jessica was not actually Australian, but only a permanent resident. Eventually, the Indonesian police said they would leave it up to the judges for sentencing.

The case quickly became the most notorious case in Indonesian history. The media gave Jessica the nickname of "The Coffee Killer," and the public interest was overwhelming in both Indonesia and Australia. The case played out like a soap opera and was covered every night on the evening news. It seemed that everyone in Indonesia had an opinion of whether Jessica was innocent or guilty.

The broadcast media was criticized for spreading insensitive rumors that Jessica was having an affair with Mirna's husband. A coffee shop in Jakarta advertised non-toxic Vietnamese iced coffee with the slogan, "What doesn't kill you makes you stronger." The Olivier restaurant became a tourist attraction for those that wanted to see where the crime took place.

The trial started on June 15, 2016, and Indonesian national television broadcast it live. Jessica's wealthy family hired Otto Hasibuan, a well-known celebrity defense lawyer. The defense team questioned the autopsy results, pointing out that they found no cyanide in any of Mirna's organs other than her stomach. They produced forensic and toxicology experts that testified there was no proof that cyanide caused her death.

Jessica took the stand in her own defense, explaining that Mirna was a friend with whom she could laugh, talk, and share secrets. She tried to play on the sympathy of the court,

> "My family has been publicly shamed, and I have been treated like the scum of the earth since the case started."

Mirna's friends and family held press conferences in attempts to sway the public option against Jessica.

The prosecution presented forty-six witnesses, including Mirna's father, husband, twin sister, and several employees from the restaurant. The prosecution presented the case with the motive of revenge. They argued that Jessica blamed Mirna for the breakup with her ex-boyfriend and the subsequent chain of events that happened in Jessica's life.

The prosecution alleged that the security camera footage showed her looking around the restaurant to see if anyone was watching while she handled the coffee. They also argued that the murder was pre-meditated - that the use of poison illustrates pre-planning. They also used the interview with Jessica's former employer, where Jessica threatened her life and the restraining order against her to show that her anger consumed her.

Ultimately, the panel of three judges agreed with the prosecution, and on October 27, 2016, after almost five months of trial, Jessica Wongso was found guilty of poisoning Mirna Salihin by putting cyanide in her coffee.

Jessica Wongso was sentenced to twenty years in prison. Jessica and her team of lawyers submitted a lengthy appeal, but both the Jakarta High Court and the Supreme Court rejected it. Jessica Wongso was left with no option but to serve the full remainder of her sentence.

Thank you for reading this bonus chapter. Please check out the rest of True Crime Case Histories: Volume 3 on Amazon.

http://truecrimecasehistories.com/book3/

THANK YOU!

Thank you for reading my first Volume of True Crime Case Histories. I truly hope you enjoyed it. If you did, I would be sincerely grateful if you would take a few minutes to write a review for me on Amazon using the link below.

http://truecrimecasehistories.com/book1/

I'd also like to encourage you to sign up for my email list for updates, discounts, and freebies on future books! I promise I'll make it worth your while with future freebies, and I'll never spam you.

http://truecrimecasehistories.com

One last thing. I would love to hear your feedback and personal thoughts on the book. I have found that many people which aren't regular readers of true crime can't handle the horrible details of stories like these. Do you think the level of detail is okay, or would you rather see it toned down a bit? Or, if you'd like to contact me for any other reason, feel free to email me at:

jason@truecrimecasehistories.com

Thanks so much,

Jason Neal

ALSO BY JASON NEAL

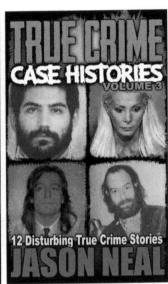

Please also check out the other volumes of this series

http://truecrimecasehistories.com/series/

ABOUT THE AUTHOR

Jason Neal is an American True Crime Author living in both London and Scottsdale, Arizona, with his Turkish-British wife. Jason started his writing career in 1989 as a music industry publisher and wrote his first true crime collection in 2019.

As a boy growing up in the 80s just south of Seattle, Jason became fascinated with true crime stories after hearing the news of the Green River Killer so close to his home. Over the coming years, he would read everything he could get his hands on about true crime and serial killers.

Now in his 40s, Jason began to assemble stories of the crimes that have fascinated him most throughout his life. He's especially obsessed by cases solved by sheer luck, amazing police work, and groundbreaking technology like early DNA cases and more recently reverse genealogy.

amazon.com/author/jason-neal

goodreads.com/JasonNeal

bookbub.com/profile/jason-neal

facebook.com/jasonnealauthor